Richard Dayringer, ThD

The Heart of Pastoral Counseling
Healing Through Relationship
Revised Edition

Pre-publication
REVIEWS,
COMMENTARIES,
EVALUATIONS . . .

"**R**ichard Dayringer's revised edition of *The Heart of Pastoral Counseling* is a book for every person's pastor and a pastor's every person. It is a book about the unique and privileged relationship between pastor and parishioners. It is based on observations and reflections of a man whose life has been spent as a dedicated pastor, professor, and therapist, both understanding and practicing that special relationship. While the book is directed to pastors, it is written in language that will help parishioners form realistic expectations of what pastors and pastoral counseling can provide."

"**R**ichard Dayringer's book is a must read for beginning pastoral counselors! He is profound in his simplicity. He teaches the basics of psychodynamics theory while reminding us it is the relationship that heals."

James E. Hightower Jr., EdD
Director, Pastoral Counseling Division,
The McFarland Institute,
New Orleans, LA

Glen W. Davidson
University Professor,
New Mexico Highlands University,
Las Vegas, NM

The Haworth Pastoral Press
An Imprint of The Haworth Press, Inc.

The Heart
of Pastoral Counseling
Healing Through Relationship

Revised Edition

THE HAWORTH PASTORAL PRESS
Pastoral Care, Ministry, and Spirituality
Richard Dayringer, ThD
Senior Editor

New, Recent, and Forthcoming Titles:

A Memoir of a Pastoral Counseling Practice by Robert L. Menz

When Life Meets Death: Stories of Death and Dying, Truth and Courage by Thomas W. Shane

The Heart of Pastoral Counseling: Healing Through Relationship, Revised Edition by Richard Dayringer

The Eight Masks of Men: A Practical Guide in Spiritual Growth for Men of the Christian Faith by Frederick G. Grosse

Hidden Addictions: A Pastoral Response to the Abuse of Legal Drugs by Bridget Clare McKeever

The Heart
of Pastoral Counseling
Healing Through Relationship

Revised Edition

Richard Dayringer, ThD

The Haworth Pastoral Press
An Imprint of The Haworth Press, Inc.
New York • London

Published by

The Haworth Pastoral Press, an imprint of The Haworth Press, Inc., 10 Alice Street, Binghamton, NY 13904-1580

Cover design by Marylouise E. Doyle.

Library of Congress Cataloging-in-Publication Data

Dayringer, Richard.
    The heart of pastoral counseling : healing through relationship / Richard Dayringer.–Rev. ed.
      p.   cm.
    Originally presented as the author's thesis (doctoral)–New Orleans Baptist Theological Seminary.
    Includes bibliographical references and index.
    ISBN 0-7890-0421-6 (alk. paper). ISBN 0-7890-0172-1 (alk. paper).
    1. Pastoral counseling. 2. Interpersonal relations–Religious aspects–Christianity. I. Title.
BV4012.2D39 1998
253′.5–dc21
                                                                         97-28387
                                                                                      CIP

CONTENTS

ABOUT THE AUTHOR

Richard Dayringer, ThD, Professor Emeritus, was formerly Professor and Director of Psychosocial Care in the Department of Medical Humanities and Professor and Chief of Behavioral Science in the Department of Family and Community Medicine at Southern Illinois University in Springfield. A pastoral psychotherapist for over thirty years, he was Director of the Department of Pastoral Care and Counseling at Baptist Memorial Hospital in Kansas City for ten years before joining the faculty at SIU School of Medicine in 1974. Dr. Dayringer also served as a pastor in Missouri, Kansas, and Louisiana prior to beginning his academic career. He has served as a consultant to various organizations, including the Department of Allied Health at the University of Texas Medical Branch, the Walter Reed Army Hospital Department of Pastoral Care, the American Correctional Chaplains Association, and the Cleveland Clinic. He has given countless international, national, and local lectures and workshops on topics such as ethical issues in medicine, depression, pastoral interventions for the bereaved, and the spiritual and psychosocial aspects of AIDS.

The author of four books including *Dealing with Depression: Five Pastoral Interventions* (The Haworth Pastoral Press, 1995) and of more than seventy professional articles, Dr. Dayringer is a member of the American Academy of Religion, an Approved Supervisor in the American Association for Marriage and Family Therapy, a Diplomate in the American Association of Pastoral Counselors, and a Certified Sex Therapist in the American Association of Sex Educators, Counselors, and Therapists. He is also a Chaplain Supervisor in the Association for Clinical Pastoral Education and a Certified Hypnotist in the Society for Clinical Hypnosis.

Preface

I have been studying the therapeutic relationship since I first discovered its importance during my doctoral studies. The evidence continues to accumulate to verify that relationship is of utmost importance in psychotherapy. It is the ubiquitous element that exists in all theories of therapy.

Pastoral counselors and psychotherapists are gifted relationship therapists. We endeavor to become all things to all people so that we might save some. We represent a relationship with God, "who comforts us in all our affliction, so that we may be able to comfort those who are in any affliction, with the comfort with which we ourselves are comforted by God" (2 Cor. 1:4).

In this revised and enlarged edition of *The Heart of Pastoral Counseling*, I have attempted to include much of the research and thought about relationship that has been published since the book was originally released in 1989. I have also tried to clarify and expand some of my own views.

Petruska Clarkson, a British clinical psychologist who is the author of twelve books, has identified five kinds of therapeutic relationship across all the major approaches to psychotherapy.

These five modalities emerged as: the *Working Alliance* as that aspect of the client-psychotherapist relationship that enables the client and therapist to work together even when the patient or client experiences strong desires to the contrary; the *transferential/countertransferential* relationship as the experience of unconscious wishes and fears transferred onto or into the therapeutic partnership; the *reparative/developmentally needed* relationship as intentional provision by the psychotherapist of a corrective, reparative, or replenishing relationship or action where the original parenting (or previous experience) was deficient, the *person-to-person* relationship as the real relationship or core relationship, as opposed to object relationship; and the *transpersonal* relationship as the timeless facet of the psychotherapeutic relationship, which is impossible to describe, but refers to the spiritual dimension of the healing relationship. It is important to remember these are not stages but states in psychotherapy or psychoanalysis, often subtly 'overlapping', in and between which a client construes his or her unique experiences.[1]

These five kinds of modalities are all discussed in this book.

I have also included a chapter on record keeping for pastoral counselors. This appears to have been a neglected area in our field of therapy. Appendixes have been added that include information about diagnosis, ethics, and membership in the American Association of Pastoral Counselors.

My prayer is that the revised edition of this book may enable both students and experienced ministers of pastoral counseling and psychotherapy to establish and maintain therapeutic relationships.

Acknowledgments

I first became interested in pastoral counseling when I was studying psychology at the University of Kansas and was thrust into the role of a pastoral counselor by certain members of the Eudora Baptist Church, which I was serving as pastor. The idea germinated in my thinking while I was doing resident studies as a graduate student at the New Orleans Baptist Theological Seminary. This was brought about by numerous statements made by Dr. Harold Rutledge, to whom I am deeply indebted for his help, criticism, and encouragement. Under his tutelage this material became my doctoral dissertation, "A Study of the Relationship in Pastoral Counseling," which established the foundation for this book.

I am also grateful to the following: John M. Price Jr., Myron C. Madden, Everett Rencer, R. Lofton Hudson, Jack R. Cooper, MD, and James G. Rice for their suggestions; to Linda Kelderman and Nadine Kraft for editorial assistance; to secretaries Hazel Smelzer, Margaret ("Peg") Moehle, Charlene Meents, and Tamara Ratsch; to my students in clinical pastoral education and my supervisees in pastoral counseling, along with my class at Midwestern Baptist Theological Seminary; to all my counselees who allowed me to test these theories and techniques with them; and most of all to my wife Janet and our children Steve, Dave, Deby, Dan, and James.

Introduction

More and more clergy are functioning as counselors. Some counsel because of choice and with training. Others have demands placed upon them by people who expect them to serve, at least at times, as counselors. This enlargement of the scope of pastoral ministry is not, as some might think, a trading of one's theological birthright for a share of psychological pottage. Counseling is a function that ministers always have performed in an informal way, as the study of the care of individuals in the history of the church verifies.[1] Today clergy are expected to counsel in a more formal way.

Various research indicates that people are more likely to discuss their problems with clergy than with any other professionals. In 1961 a study reported that 42 percent of the people who sought professional help for their personal problems consulted clergy. Only 29 percent consulted physicians in general, while 18 percent saw psychiatrists or psychologists, and 10 percent social agencies or marriage clinics.[2] In 1967 another study found that 34 percent of respondents anticipated using the clergy as a resource, and 4 percent actually used them.[3] A national survey completed in 1976 found that 39 percent of the people surveyed reported that they sought help from pastors; no other professional was selected as frequently.[4] In a Gallup study published in 1993, 66 percent of the general population indicated they "would prefer a professional counselor who is religious."[5] The demands that people make of clergy will not allow them to decide whether they will serve as counselors. The question is, how well will their ministry of counseling be performed when requested?

Psychotherapists help many of their clients achieve a measure of psychological and personal adjustment even though they subscribe to a variety of theories, treatment methods, and techniques. One reason why differing schools of psychotherapy can achieve similar results is that they are built on the therapeutic relationship. Jerome D. Frank, who has doctorates in both medicine and psychology, has

1

stated unequivocally that "every successful theory establishes a relationship."[6]

When I was in training at East Louisiana State Hospital, I heard a psychiatrist lecture on the subject of psychotherapy to numerous groups of graduate students from the disciplines of psychiatry, psychology, and social work. He usually began by asking the class, "What is the essence of psychotherapy?" In one form or another the answer invariably came back: "The essence of psychotherapy is the relationship between the counselor and the counselee." Helen Harris Perlman, in her book *Relationships: The Heart of Helping People,* wrote, "What is the common element, the red thread, that seems to run through every successful effort by one person to influence another in benign and enabling ways? The answer seems to be 'relationship.' "[7] Moreover, Clarkson wrote: "A wealth of studies demonstrates that it is the relationship between the client and the psychotherapist, more than any other factor, which determines the effectiveness of psychotherapy" (1997).[8] Therefore, this interpersonal relationship, which is the apparent vehicle of therapy, should be the first subject of concern in pastoral counseling.

The purpose of this book is to investigate the therapeutic relationship in pastoral counseling and to determine what contribution it makes. We will examine ways in which this relationship might be used to a greater extent by pastors not only in counseling, but also in other interpersonal relationships with parishioners.

The relationship in counseling consists of the communicative, emotional, and status aspects of a counselor's behavior toward the client. In their book *The Psychotherapy Relationship,* William and June Snyder define relationship as "the reciprocity of various sets of affective attitudes which two or more persons hold toward each other in psychotherapy."[9] The term has other definitions, but in this study it is used to refer to interpersonal activity that is common to all types of counseling.

The word relationship is often preceded—as it will be in this book—by the adjective "therapeutic," which describes a curative or healing process. "Relationship" may also be modified at times by other descriptive adjectives such as "counseling," "psychotherapeutic," or "helping."

I have drawn from the disciplines of psychiatry, psychology, marriage counseling, family therapy, and social work as well as pastoral counseling, since professionals in all these areas have theorized at times about relationship. A growing mass of theory and research concerning the relationship will be reviewed in this book. I am convinced that the therapeutic relationship is the essence of all psychotherapy, including pastoral counseling. Unfortunately, little systematic study has been done to date with the pastoral counseling relationship.

Some major challenges emerged during my research. As late as 1961 the term *relationship,* or *interpersonal relationship,* was considered "a psychological unknown."[10] Such agnosticism is unwarranted, because relationship is a known and definable entity. In this book relationship will be defined as "the spontaneous and earned reciprocity of affective attitudes that persons hold toward each other." This definition will be developed and explained in Chapter 2.

Another challenge is distinguishing relationship from transference and countertransference. In theory these phenomena can be distinguished rather easily. Relationship is conscious, arising from the current interaction between persons, while transference and countertransference are unconscious, arising out of the past and out of previous relationships. Yet, in practice—that is, in the process of counseling—an immediate and accurate distinction of one reaction from the other is sometimes almost impossible.

A third challenge was my having to reconcile my thesis with two pieces of research reported in the journals that somewhat minimize the significance of relationship. First, Joseph W. Eaton wrote an incisive review of the development of theory concerning the relationship in social work. He concluded that relationship may not always be enough to bring about the desired changes.[11] He thought that environmental manipulation might occasionally be needed.

Second, Donald M. Sundland and Edwin N. Barker[12] set out to test the conclusions reported in the well-known 1950 research of F. E. Fiedler, a clinical psychologist.[13] While the studies did contest some of Fiedler's findings and some aspects of his experimental method, it is noteworthy that Fiedler's first discovery—that representatives from different therapeutic theories tend to establish approximately the same kind of therapeutic relationship—was not questioned.

I have attempted in Part I to describe the nature of pastoral counseling relationships and how they are helpful to people. In Part II, I set forth the dimensions of pastoral counseling relationships. In Part III, I distinguish between friendships and therapeutic relationships and also delineate how pastoral relationships may be generalized outside the therapeutic hour into general pastoral work.

PART I:
WHAT IS THE PASTORAL
COUNSELING RELATIONSHIP?

Many therapists agree on the importance of the therapeutic relationship, even though they have different educational backgrounds and subscribe to different schools of psychotherapeutic thought. One writer summarized this conclusion: "The key to the influence of psychotherapy on the patient is in his relationship with the therapist. Wherever psychotherapy is accepted as a significant enterprise, this statement is so widely subscribed to as to become trite."[1]

Relationship is the essence of counseling being done by clergy. To be sure, such counseling may incorporate a wide variety of methods and techniques, but the essential component that brings about the resolution of difficulties is the therapeutic relationship between the minister and the counselee. Since relationship is considered to have this importance in all psychotherapy, and since the clergy's vocation centers in interpersonal relationships both human and divine, I attempt here to set forth an adequate concept of the pastoral counseling relationship.

Chapter 1

A Philosophical Foundation for the Pastoral Counseling Relationship

The assumptions and attitudes of relationship-centered pastoral counseling are based on Hebraic-Christian thought and rooted deeply in American democratic philosophy and cultural traditions. The blending of the eighteenth-century emphasis on universal human rights with the nineteenth-century values of uniqueness and individuality has created a rich background for this counseling philosophy. Dayton G. Van Deusen summarizes a basic assumption for this philosophy of counseling by stating:

> Most of life is constituted of relationship. Gravity is a relationship of bodies, matter a relationship of particles, fire a relationship of substances, logic a relationship of ideas, truth a relationship of realities, love a relationship of spirits, religion a relationship of being.[1]

Emotional difficulties are usually rooted in problems in interpersonal relationships. Conversely, people are mentally healthy to the extent to which they are aware of and able to handle their interpersonal relationships. As noted psychotherapist C. H. Patterson argued, the "human relationship is the most powerful psychological behavior modifier known to man."[2]

In this concept of counseling, it is important not to make conscious the infantile frustrations (Sigmund Freud) or the guiding purpose (Alfred Adler) or the archetypal unconscious (Carl G. Jung), but rather the interpersonal relationship itself. Of course the factors just named are to be considered, but they are subordinate to the actual moment of experience. The therapeutic experience is valuable in its honesty and creativity—benefits that enable counselees to enrich themselves. I agree with pastoral counselor Charles Gerkin, who writes: "The primary goal of a therapeutic relationship is . . . the facilitation of changes in the self in relation to its fragmentation and in authenticity."[3]

Otto Rank, the philosophical psychologist who defected from Freud, brought the therapeutic concept of relationship into view as a determining consideration, both in therapy and in personality development more generally. He emphasized relationship rather than interpretation in counseling. Rank's approach was novel because material produced during analysis was to be understood not by reference to the past but only as it related to the relationship between client and therapist. Therefore Rank's therapy remained almost entirely on the feeling level, where emotional experiences are central and where spontaneous expressions of unique individuality are complemented as a sign of a growing will and as a way of understanding oneself.[4]

Such a therapeutic relationship is also the essence of more recent theoretical approaches to psychotherapy, including behavior modification, Gestalt therapy, object relations therapy, transactional analysis, and systems theory in marriage and family therapy. These theories do not all emphasize insight as the key to personality and behavior change. The interpersonal relationship between counselors and clients is the basis of therapy.

AN UNDERSTANDING OF INDIVIDUALS

Ministerial counselors naturally look to the teachings of Jesus Christ for an understanding of people. They also study in the fields of philosophy, psychology, and sociology. My understanding of individuals, a synthesis of these influences forged with personal experience, can be summed up in these axioms:

1. *Individuals have intrinsic worth and dignity.* This is the "image of God" in persons. It is apparent in the ability to communicate intelligibly, to transcend oneself, to contemplate the future, to choose responsibly, and to experience humor.
2. *Individuals have supreme value.* People have supreme value over institutional, moralistic, or any other values. Individuals should

not be underrated either in terms of their complete selves or in their place in the society of which they are a part. People should not use one another merely as a means to an end, but should relate to one another according to Martin Buber's notion of "I and Thou."[5] Human beings constitute God's supreme creation.

3. *Individuals have needs.* Every person has certain inherent needs. The catalogs of these needs (motives, instincts, drives) may vary. Ecclesiasticus 39:26 reads, "The basic necessities of human life are water and fire and iron and salt and wheat flour and milk and honey, the blood of the grape and oil and clothing."[6] The following list probably encompasses most basic needs: air, drink and food, rest and sleep, movement and exercise, cleanliness, fellowship and communication, love and sex. These things are not optional; they are necessary for survival and well-being. The optional things are the methods people employ to fulfill these needs. The well-known hierarchy of needs by Abraham Maslow may be studied in Figure 1.1.[7]

FIGURE 1.1. Maslow's Hierarchy of Needs

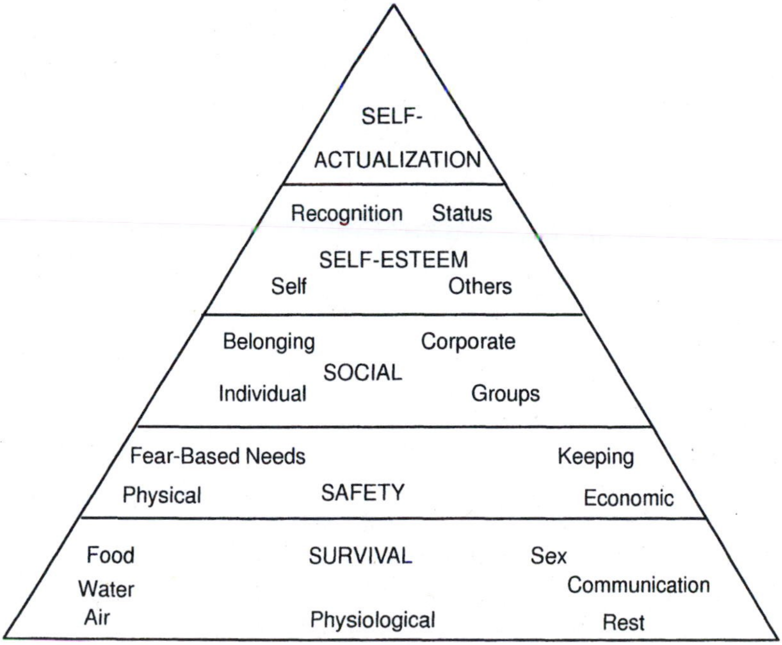

4. *Individuals have goals.* People place different values on things, and in striving for the things they value, they set goals for themselves. People cannot be understood psychologically apart from these goals, because mental processes and their resultant physical activity are always oriented toward goals that offer some promise of value.

5. *Individuals relate to one another.* Relationality assumes the need for interaction as the state in which individuals realize their personhood. Paul Johnson noted that it "is doubtful whether human personality would develop at all if one were completely isolated from other persons."[8] Virtually everyone born into the world has the capacity for forming interpersonal relationships. People seem to need to have such interactions daily. Even voluntarily denying interpersonal relationships out of a desire for intense and prolonged meditation or study, as in monasticism, seems unnatural and can be very difficult. Prolonged isolation is considered so formidable that solitary confinement is used as a form of special punishment in prisons.

6. *Individuals have freedom.* Each person has the inherent right to make decisions and to lead a private life. Individuals have the potential to choose wisely and to live a self-directed, self-fulfilled, and self-transcended life.[9] People even have the right to be wrong. Of course, this freedom can be controlled or curbed by social institutions such as government.

7. *Individuals have responsibility.* Each person is responsible for each personal choice made. People are responsible for their lives and responsible to God and to their fellow humans for every decision. Thus people are responsible for participating in and maintaining their relationships, both human and divine.

8. *Individuals grow through love.* For centuries love has been the theme of prophets, teachers, and poets. More recently, behavioral scientists have suggested that life without love is fatally flawed. The unwanted child, the juvenile delinquent, the neurotic adult, and the senile elder represent a straight line of loveless despair. Paul Johnson points out that when love is available, tragedies like these may be avoided, but when love is lacking, psychological growth is stunted or distorted.[10]

9. *Individuals have access to divine relationship.* As they mature in their understanding of human relationships, people often become aware of the potential for developing a personal relationship with God. Guilt may motivate people to seek such a relationship because of the divine forgiveness that is implied within it.

These nine axioms represent some basic philosophical assumptions necessary for understanding people. Next I will discuss diagnostic and therapeutic ways for pastoral counselors to understand their clients.

AN ECLECTIC VIEW OF COUNSELING

Counselors who describe their theoretical position as "eclectic" have selected what they think is best from various systems of counseling. Taken literally, this ascription seems to place such counselors in a rather favorable light, assuming that a composite of what is best from many sources might reasonably be expected to turn out well. In the field of counseling or psychotherapy, however, eclecticism formerly had unfavorable connotations. Until recently eclectic counselors were considered by their professional colleagues to be either muddled or "unsystematic." Most therapists were strongly urged to identify with the "party line" of a particular therapeutic club.

Frederick C. Thorne, who has doctorates in both medicine and psychology, has written: "There is an urgent need for a comprehensive integration of all scientific data into a 'system' of practice which would be genuinely eclectic and provide a basis for the standardization of practice throughout the world."[11] Thorne attempted to set forth such a "system," but it has not been accepted as the standard for counseling around the world. Perhaps the truly urgent need is for *all individual counselors* to integrate comprehensively the scientific data available to them into an eclectic "system" of practice that fits their personality. This system would provide the basis for each counselor's practice anywhere in the world. In other words, since the theory of individual differences implies that theory and practice will be personalized, counselors might as well admit it.

Modern psychology has spawned a large number of systems or schools of psychotherapy that have originated from diverse philosophical and methodological viewpoints. Robert Harper easily identified three dozen systems,[12] but more than 250 different therapies have been described.[13] Patterson, however, argued as early as 1971 that the "days of 'schools' in counseling and psychotherapy are drawing to a close."[14] In 1986, he published his book, *The Therapeutic Relationship: Foundations for an Eclectic Psychotherapy*.

William Oglesby suggests a helpful grouping of three types of psychotherapies: those that give priority to *knowing,* those to *doing,* and those to *being*. Psychoanalysis and transactional analysis are *knowing* therapies; reality therapy and behavior therapy are *doing* therapies; and client-centered and Gestalt therapies are *being* therapies.[15]

By contrast, J. Harold Ellens divides all theories into four types: rational, emotional, relational, and biological. Rational-emotive therapy would be an example of the first, client-centered therapy the second, Gestalt therapy the third, and behavior therapy the fourth.[16]

A comparison of these systems of psychotherapy reveals considerable variation in aspects of counseling that could affect the counselor-client relationship. For example, there is a difference of opinion as to how ambiguous the role of the counselor should be. Freudians are at one end of this continuum and directive counselors at the other. A second difference is counselor warmth or aloofness. Here Carl Rogers and Freud stand at opposite ends of the spectrum. Third, some tell clients to work at remembering the past (Freud), and some instruct them to aim at solving present problems (Frederick Perls). A fourth difference is the activity or passivity of particular counselors; this mode ranges from directive counselors to the Rogerians. Fifth, some counselors focus more on the affect (emotional tone) of their client than on cognition. Rogerians and Freudians join at one end of this continuum and the cognitive therapists at the other. A comparison of four psychotherapeutic systems is shown in Figure 1.2.

Eclectic counselors, realizing the current limitations of systematic theory, struggle to integrate and rationalize the elements and conflicts among the theories of psychotherapy on the basis of their personal experience. They try assiduously to organize their observations and hypotheses into a flexible but workable and consistent position that they are willing to revise in the light of new factual data.

FIGURE 1.2. Comparison of Therapeutic Relationship in Five Therapy Modalities

Therapy Modality	Aspect of Relationship Emphasized	Therapeutic Techniques	Therapist Stance	Therapist Role	Task of Client
Psychoanalytic	Transference-Counter Transference with emphasis on affect	Interpretation of transference	Neutral	Surrogate parent	Free-association
Client-Centered	Real relationship	Unconditional positive regard	Authentic	Professional friend	Self-acceptance
Behavioral	Working relationship	Changing maladaptive behavior with graded assignments	Directive	Trainer	Modify behavior
Cognitive	Teaching relationship	Discriminate faulty thinking with record-keeping	Confrontive	Teacher	Qualify thinking
Systems	Joining the family	Advice, homework, paradox	Active, indirect	Coach	Change family relationships

By 1982, one study indicated that the majority of psychotherapists were eclectic.[17] The following authors, whose works are listed in the bibliography, have stated their eclectic positions: Lawrence M. Brammer and Everett L. Shostrom, C. W. Brister, Robert R. Carkhuff and Bernard G. Berenson, Albert Ellis, Jerome D. Frank, Frieda Fromm-Reichman, Bernard G. Guerney, Jr., Harrison V. Ingham and Lenore R. Love, Edgar N. Jackson, J. C. Norcross, Wayne E. Oates, C. H. Patterson, William U. and June B. Snyder, Bernard Steinzor, Frederick C. Thorne, Leona E. Tyler, and Leslie D. Weatherhead.[18]

Some writers in the field of pastoral counseling advocate an eclectic approach for ministerial counselors. Wayne Oates, for instance, writes that his approach at any given moment is gauged by the kind of self-confrontation going on in the therapeutic relationship. He believes that to use any particular approach exclusively in every situation is to become a slave of that method. He does not suggest a "willy-nilly eclecticism," but the making of clinical decisions based on adequate knowledge of the principles of interpersonal relationships.[19] C. W. Brister writes, "Concerned about counseling *relationships,* ministers generally do not hold rigidly to one counseling system or therapeutic technique."[20] Edgar N. Jackson reasoned as follows:

> Because no one school or philosophy has an adequate concept of human personality from the Christian point of view, it is essential to draw from varied sources and to develop an amalgamation that serves the purpose of the parish minister.[21]

The following paragraphs will trace the history of early studies of the therapeutic relationship.

In a number of studies, eclecticism and the ubiquitous counselor-client relationship have become the masked "tag team" opponents with which researchers have wrestled. In the study cited earlier, F. E. Fiedler found that therapists adhering to different systems agreed highly as to the nature and importance of the therapeutic relationship. He also concluded that there was more agreement between experienced practitioners of different systems than between more experienced and less experienced adherents of the same school of thought. Furthermore, Fiedler's study of recorded interviews revealed that experts in different systems created relationships more similar to each other than did experts and novices within the same system.[22]

Other research either based on or similar to Fiedler's study followed. One study concluded that (1) the changes seen by clients as a result of therapy did not differ in a way that was attributable to their having been treated under different systems; and (2) the changes experienced by clients and the factors in therapist behavior seen as responsible for the changes were related to each other regardless of system affiliation.[23]

Another study proposed that the basic elements of all therapies are as follows: (1) rapport between therapist and client; (2) acceptance (or appreciation) of the client by the therapist; (3) support of the client; (4) superior status of the therapist; and (5) a controlled and limited interaction.[24]

Still another researcher compared the way clients and therapists pictured the ideal therapeutic relationship both before and after therapy. This study found that the more experienced therapists had highly similar concepts of the ideal relationship. In successful cases the actual relationship became increasingly more like the ideal in the therapists' and clients' perceptions.[25]

Over time, and after much research, eclectic counselors have gained wide acceptance among their psychotherapeutic colleagues in psychiatry, psychology, social work, and marriage and family counseling. In fact, a new journal, the *Journal of Integrative and Eclectic Psychotherapy,* was inaugurated in 1987. Albert Ellis has stated: "In writing about the future of counseling and psychotherapy, I shall naturally take a biased view and hold that its future will largely be eclectic and integrative as that is the way therapy is developing" (1997).[26]

Many counseling ministers also find eclecticism to their liking and use clues from varied therapeutic methods. Pastoral psychotherapy needs a systematic prescriptive eclecticism. Such an eclecticism would need to be different from an eclectic orientation that remains open to every new development to prevent pastoral psychotherapists from falling prey to fads. Competent therapists must have certain knowledge as a foundation. They must know, for example, that psychopharmacologists have demonstrated that lithium carbonate is strongly indicated for a client with a bipolar affective disorder in a florid manic phase; and that a client with encrusted obsessive- compulsive symptoms will respond best to behavioral therapy.

In my own ministry of pastoral counseling I employ many theories and techniques of therapy. I began by studying psychoanalysis and I found that, even to this day, when reading Freud I remember more dreams than usual. At the New Orleans Baptist Theological Seminary, I was introduced to client-centered therapy. Both theories continue to influence my counseling. One by one I became thoroughly familiar with the theories of transactional analysis, Gestalt, behavior therapy, cognitive therapy, and family systems.[28] The counseling techniques suggested in these theories have intrigued me, and I have not been reluctant to use them if they felt comfortable and fit my personality. Yet the compass that has guided me through the forest of these and other psychotherapeutic theories has been a high regard for the therapeutic relationship. Such focus has helped me fit theory and technique to particular clients.

A THEOLOGY OF RELATIONSHIP

From the interpersonal point of view, the religious life is a search for divine relationship. One of a person's basic needs is for a responsive encounter. From the beginning to the end of life, the finite person, being incomplete in himself or herself, reaches out to relate to others. The meeting of a human being with the person of God in a religious encounter enhances the value of the individual and enlarges one's meaning in life.

Several theological principles regarding the meaning, purpose, and function of the pastoral counselor appear to be significant: (1) God created persons for relationship both human and divine; (2) Christ demonstrated divine and human relationships at their best; (3) humanity has recognized the need for personal interaction, but has generally questioned the life-fulfilling qualities of a relationship with God; and (4) God implements a relationship with one person through the help of another person.

God's Creation

God created people with the capacity for a tangible relationship with other persons and an intangible relationship with himself. All people have a God-given freedom to choose when, how, and with whom to relate. People even choose whether or not to relate either to God or to others at all! The central characteristic of the relationship that God offers people, according to the Bible, is one of grace (cf. Rom. 5:1-12; Luke 15:11- 24; 1 John 3:1-2, 16, 24).

The purpose of a theology of relationship is to make persons aware of their relationship to God as Creator. Such a theory is quite relevant, because no part of life is beyond its reach; it assumes that the activities of all people are important to God. The theory of relationship is not remote from real life. It is engaged in the day-to-day struggle of persons to find meaning in the multiplicity of selves, the turmoil of human relations, and the encounter with the cosmic forces that surround them.

Life is dynamic. A theology of relationship assumes that life is a process of achieving identities that sustain and move each person toward true fulfillment. The ultimate in right relationships is the quest for the will of God within the relationships of life.

Christ's Demonstration

Jesus of Nazareth presented the most profound demonstration of how to enter meaningful relationships with God and people. Jesus expressed his theology of relationship by encouraging his followers to practice the truths he revealed.

Jesus was the incarnation of the minister's ideal as a counselor. The Gospel accounts of his life give an amazing record of one who had a unique insight into the needs and problems of people. Jesus "knew what was in everyone" (John 2:25). Mankind has made a mark of honor the taunt of Jesus' enemies: that he was a "friend of sinners."[29]

Insisting on the necessity of correcting inner attitudes, Jesus was never willing to accept emphasis on external behavior. He was vitally concerned with what was going on in the depths of people. In so doing, he emphasized a sacred element in personality.

Religion was to Christ a matter of active relationship. Indeed, he summed up all Scripture in terms of relationship when he said:

> "Love the Lord your God with all your heart and with all your soul and with all your mind." This is the greatest and first

commandment. And a second is like it: "You shall love your neighbor as yourself." On these two commandments all the Law and Prophets hang. (Matt. 22:37-40)

Jesus's focus is evident in his three parables on broken relationships in Luke 15. The *coin* was lost by accident. It had meaning only in relationship. When found and returned to its right relationship, its meaning returned. This also seems true of the person who gets separated from the social structure that gives life meaning. The *sheep* became lost by carelessness. The sustaining relationship was broken by careless wandering. The concerned person was interested in restoring the essential relationship so that life could function as intended. The *son* became lost by choice. Separated from the meaningful structures of relationship, he came to himself and reestablished himself within the proper framework.[30]

Humanity's Partial Recognition

Most people try to express their uniqueness in some way. Many wish to separate themselves from others because problems frequently arise from humans being in close proximity to one another. Emotional injuries often occur to people through personal interaction.

Nevertheless, people recognize the need for relationships. Throughout history individuals have lived in families, tribes, and communities. This recognition of the need for community is behind the Hebrew psychological phrase used for penal solitude; such people were "cut off from the land of the living."[31]

Thus individuals are pulled in two directions simultaneously: toward separation and toward relationship. At the core of this tension is the knowledge that the very consciousness of being a person is greatly enhanced by entering into relationship with another.

Yet people sometimes deny the fulfilling qualities of a divine relationship. External conflicts with one another and internal disturbances over past errors and future goals continually harass people, so much so that they often seek self-justification. Once discovering that they cannot justify themselves, people occasionally move more dependently toward one another, looking for a savior in the human form of parent, spouse, superior, or friend, or in such groups as the family, club, state, or church.

God's Implementation

God has used people in their relationships with one another as instruments for the revelation of himself. People have sought divine encounter in a direct, vertical fashion that would augment their independence even as they seek God's assistance. More realistically, however, human relationships often prove to be the channel through which a person receives impressions and concepts of the intangible and the transcendent. Thus human interaction many times comes first, and the divine level of relationship is perceived through the human level.

Interpersonal conversation, when successful, involves the acceptance of both otherness and togetherness. This is true, according to Johnson, of every real meeting of person with person. All people participate in a partnership with the individuals who confront them in active relationships. Psychological and religious fulfillment is not in one person or the other alone, nor in both of them crowded into one collective mass that submerges their identities. Rather, fulfillment lies in the dialogue, between them where they live on speaking terms together. In genuine dialogue, people communicate openly and honestly and contribute a part of their own spirits. Thus every person stands in relation to other persons, and these relationships are essential to religious life.[32]

People usually approach ministerial counselors to seek theological answers to the dilemmas of their human existence. Ministers offer people a relationship with a person who tends to perceive all things theologically. A minister can try to help clients to faith by going down into the morass in which they are mired in the quest for life's meaning. Charles William Stewart wrote that a minister "knows he must descend into hell oft-times with the parishioner before he can ascend into the heaven of cured and righted relationship with God."[33]

Individuals who benefit from a personal relationship are helped by the love present in it. Nothing is especially transforming about the cold imparting of truth. People who have been emotionally injured through personal interaction are probably best healed through interpersonal relationship. Van Deusen argues, "Nothing will fill the needs of both sides of the mediating process, the human and the divine, except relationship."[34]

Dietrich Bonhoeffer, the martyred German theologian, suggested a penultimate form of ministry that is meaningful to the pastoral counseling relationship. The penultimate includes all the things that aid in providing the route over which God travels in coming to people. However, the next to the last word can only be known when the last word is spoken. The preparation of the way to divine-human encounter is known as a preparation only in retrospect. God's self-sufficiency, self-initiation, and self-revelation serve as the main reasons for adopting a penultimate form of ministry. In counseling relationships, ministers do not bring God's word to others. Perhaps they prepare the way, but God comes on his own initiative.[35]

The New Testament teachings on the Holy Spirit of God contain indispensable wisdom for the practice of pastoral counseling. Especially relevant is the Revised Standard Version's translation of the Greek name of the *paraclete* as "the counselor." The Holy Spirit is, in truth, the counselor in every interpersonal relationship.[36] Traditionally this is the image of the pastoral relationship as analogous to the incarnation of God in Christ. Knowing that the counselee is actually in the hands of God helps the minister to be more secure in the role of counselor. The Holy Spirit is always at work in a relationship, especially in the communication gap that exists between the minister and the counselee. The Holy Spirit is also present to guide memory, interpretation, and inspiration.

An ultimate goal of Christian counselors is to enable their counselees to find divine forgiveness and redemption through God-in-Christ. The very divine-human relationship for which people hope was established by the vicarious death of Christ.

Chapter 2

A Theoretical Framework
for the Pastoral
Counseling Relationship

It is appropriate now to take those things known or supposed about the curative powers of relationship and correlate them with the discipline of pastoral counseling. This theoretical framework is built on the preceding discussions of the philosophical concepts of an understanding of individuals, an eclectic view of counseling, and a theology of relationships.

A DEFINITIVE DESCRIPTION

A definitive description of the pastoral counseling relationship seems to be a better goal than a precise definition. The phrase *pastoral counseling relationship* will be broken into two segments. I will explain first what is meant by pastoral counseling and then discuss it in terms of the relationship.

Pastoral Counseling

Actually, the descriptive adjective "pastoral" in the phrase *pastoral counseling* causes some misunderstanding. Currently, the public appears to prefer to favor the term "spiritual" to replace or update the historical term pastoral. The word *pastor* is used, along with *priest* and *preacher*, to refer to particular functions in the ministry. The terms *clergy* or *minister* refer more generally to the professional religious practitioner. Using the word *pastor*, with its inference of a minister serving a local congregation, excludes many theologically trained professionals. These professionals include ministers of religious education, music, pastoral care, and youth, as well as chaplains in a variety of institutional and military settings, and ministers who function in religious counseling centers. Nevertheless, pastor has a traditional connotation of guiding and shepherding people anywhere. This idea is contained in the phrase *pastoral counseling.*

In their book *The Context of Pastoral Counseling,* Seward Hiltner and Lowell Colston include the following in their definition of the term *pastoral:* (1) a special area of theological expertness brought to the relationship, along with knowledge and skill about counseling; (2) acknowledgment that the person seeking help has very likely come to the counselor because of having a presenting problem presumed to relate to the realm of theological expertness; and (3) this special area of expertness has to be related to the needs of the total person.[1]

The term *counseling* began to be used in relation to the work of ministers around 1930. Since *psychotherapy* refers to a therapist expert in the study of the human psyche, *theological therapist* implies a therapist expert in the study of God. The word *therapy* is derived from the Greek noun meaning "servant" and the verb "to wait." Fortunately the word in English has no verb form and has never suggested the idea of doing something to somebody. Rather, therapy represents a process going on—observed, understood, and assisted—but not applied. An apparently growing number of clergy who have specialized in pastoral counseling seem to prefer the term *pastoral psychotherapist* to distinguish what the specialist does from the counseling done by clergy generally.[2] Deductively, the phrase *theological therapy relationship* is the most accurate of all phrases for the subject of this study. Nevertheless, the widespread use of the phrase *pastoral counseling* to include all therapy done by clergy renders it sufficient.

Though similar to secular counseling, pastoral counseling is unique. First, it is different because only the theologically oriented engage in it. Only those who have experienced a divine call—one that has been recognized and affirmed by a religious group—and then have studied theology and have been ordained or endorsed to a ministry of counseling can be said to practice pastoral counseling.

Second, ordination or endorsement symbolizes the authority given to the pastor by God through the religious group. This authority points beyond itself to God's power. Third, the clergy's social and symbolic role, which is conferred by ordination, is confirmed by society. This role has a long and historical tradition that empowers clergy to perform public rituals, celebrations, and rites of passage for others such as baptism, weddings, communion, and funerals.

Fourth, clergy counsel within a context that relates them to their churches. Each church is a fellowship of self-selected people who embody a tradition of beliefs and practices that relate to their eternal destiny. Fifth, counseling ministers are responsible and accountable for their behavior, not only to their clients and their communities, but also to the church and to God. Sixth, ministers assume the presence and guidance of the Holy Spirit during counseling. Seventh, clergy have available certain resources such as prayer, Scripture, church ordinances, public worship, service projects, and educational or fellowship groups that they can use to support their clients. Eighth, clergy are committed to certain values such as confidentiality, honesty, respect for individuals as God's creation, and accountability to God for behavior. People who choose to consult with clergy about their problems often do so because they respect such values and cannot be certain that secular therapists subscribe to them. Ninth, clergy also maintain counseling goals that include divine forgiveness and redemption rather than just human relief.

All these distinctions imply that the process of pastoral counseling will encompass some activities that other forms of therapy often omit. These include, for example, exploring religious history, evaluating biases and stereotypes of biblical teaching, probing into the meaning of the marriage vows, considering how the fear of death motivates behavior, inquiring into the client's ethics, and considering the need for confession of sin, for receiving divine forgiveness, and for seeking God's blessing.

Relationship

In their book *Therapeutic Psychology*, Brammer and Shostrom conclude that the "quality of the relationship determines not only the nature of the personal exchanges but whether counseling will continue at all."[3] These two recognized psychologists noted that they were convinced more and more that the relationship in counseling is a curative agent. John Patton stated, "If any healing occurs through pastoral counseling, it occurs through relationship."[4] Carl Rogers also lays great stress "upon the therapeutic relationship itself as a growth experience."[5] Helen Harris Perlman, a social worker, wrote an entire chapter on the definition and ramifications of relationship in her noteworthy book, *Relationship: The Heart of Helping People.*[6] Sheldon Cashdan's book *Object Relations Therapy: Using the Relationship* describes a treatment approach that places maximum emphasis on the therapist-patient relationship.[7] Michael Kahn called Heinz Kohut "a relationship therapist."[8]

Rogers makes a clear distinction between relationship and transference. For him, relationship "is something which is mutual and appropriate, where transference or countertransference are phenomena which are characteristically one-way and inappropriate to the realites of the situation."[9]

Relationship, in contrast to transference and countertransference, refers to the conscious, voluntary, realistic, appropriate, rational, legitimate, and earned responses of both counselor and client to one another in their current interaction. It is the emotional force that comes into operation between two or more people because of their communicative behavior. *Relationship, then, is the spontaneous and earned reciprocity of affective attitudes which persons hold toward each other.* The difficulty in distinguishing relationship from transference is, of course, similar to the practical difficulties of differentiating the conscious from the subconscious and unconscious material in verbal and nonverbal communication. Conceptually this distinction can be made, but in the practice of counseling, separating relationship from transference is at times almost impossible.

Many others also have taken the position that transference and relationship are not the same. Jung wrote that "once the projections are recognized as such . . . the transference is at an end, and the problem of the individual relationships begins."[10] Rank said that "the therapeutic relationship represents an actual feeling experience. . . . We do not need to go back into the past."[11] Rogers stated that his "therapy places greater stress upon the immediate situation than upon the individual's past."[12]

Therapists from such divergent viewpoints as psychoanalysis, neo-Freudian analysis, directive counseling, and client-centered counseling have wide agreement as to the importance of a good relationship for a successful outcome in therapy. Despite the differences in the client-therapist relationship in the various schools of psychotherapy, many scholars have argued that it is the relationship itself that is the common element among different therapies.[13] Yet few have made empirical or theoretical investigations into the nature of the pastoral counseling relationship.

Arthur H. Becker did complete one such experimental study on the function of the pastoral counseling relationship. The specific focus of this research was to determine the impact of religious concerns on the therapeutic relationship in pastoral counseling. Becker used a modified "Q-sort" technique employing a series of items prepared by Fiedler that had been sorted by psychotherapists of leading "schools" of therapy. He gave eleven pastoral counselors this series to sort. The sortings were then compared with those of the psychotherapists. A second series of seventy-five items was constructed that included the dimensions of trust and religious climate. The eleven pastoral counselors then sorted this latter grouping, and it was compared with the results of their sortings of the series without the religious factors present. This was to determine the impact of these factors on the relationship. Becker then constructed an interview analysis schedule on the basis of the sorting of the seventy-five items. Forty-four hospital pastoral interviews—twenty-two known to be "good," and twenty-two known to be "poor"—were rated by four judges using the schedule to determine the quality of the relationship, the fulfillment of functions, and the achieving of goals in each.

Becker listed the following findings and conclusions:

1. Psychotherapists and pastoral counselors agreed extensively as to the nature of the ideal therapeutic relationship when considering dimensions of communication, emotional distance, and status of therapist.
2. The pastoral counseling relationship has five dimensions: communication, status, trust, emotional distance, and religious climate.

3. Both the secular and the pastoral counseling relationship have three major functions: the relationship gratifies basic needs, serves as an occasion for social learning, and acts as a corrective experience and model for interpersonal relationships. In the pastoral counseling relationship there were, however, specific religious overtones evident in each of these functions.

4. Four major goals are common to both types of relationship: personal integration, self-acceptance, restoration of wholesome interpersonal relationships, and discovery of new meaning in life. In pastoral counseling these were seen in the light of ultimate religious values.

5. The religious dimension of pastoral counseling took precedence over all others in the "Q-sorts" when both religious and nonreligious items were considered together. The impact of the religious dimension exceeded, in order, the effect of communication, trust, status, and emotional distance.

6. Pastoral counselors closely integrated the communication dimension with the religious dimension. The items considered most typical of the ideal pastoral counseling relationship deal with communication of the acceptance and forgiveness of God and the awareness of the redemptive processes of God in the pastoral relationship.[14]

A second noteworthy study was done by Fiedler. He began with the assumption that expertness rather than allegiance to a certain system of psychotherapy determined the type of goal therapists set for the counselor-client relationship. All therapists endeavor to create an ideal relationship. If only one type of relationship is actually therapeutic, then experienced therapists should be in accord on the concept of an ideal relationship.

Fiedler used ten judges in his experiment. There were three therapists from an analytic orientation, three from a client-centered orientation, one from the Adlerian school, and three laypeople. These judges were asked to describe the ideal therapeutic relationship by means of the "Q-sort" technique. Seventy-five statements, descriptive of a possible aspect of relationship, were sorted by each judge into seven categories ranging from most characteristic of an ideal relationship to least characteristic. The results indicated that all the judges tended to describe the ideal relationship in similar terms. There was a higher correlation between experts who were regarded as good therapists, regardless of orientation, than between experts and nonexperts within the same orientation. The fact that even lay-people described the ideal therapeutic relationship in terms which correlated highly with those of the experts suggested that the best therapeutic relationship may be related to good interpersonal relationships in general.[15]

The pastoral counselor normally enters a relationship with a religious perspective. For clergy, God's love is involved in the relationship, undergirding both minister and client. The pastoral counseling relationship, like the psychotherapeutic one, attempts to set up a good society in miniature. Pastoral counselors try to provide the kind of interpersonal relationship that does not obscure, but rather magnifies and illuminates the relationship God offers individuals. Thus the ministerial counseling relationship, like all others, is the spontaneous and earned reciprocity of affective attitudes between counselor and client.

For the pastoral counselor, this relationship is used to help resolve the conflicts within the client's relationship to self, to others, or to God. These conflicts are expressed negatively as disability, distress, and dread. No matter what their orientation, therapists try to improve a client's ability to establish mutually satisfying relationships with others.

Pastoral counselors have the additional goal of enabling their counselees to experience God's grace. In his study Becker found that pastoral counselors held several goals in common with psychotherapists: (1) personality integration; (2) self-acceptance; (3) restoration of wholesome interpersonal relationships; and (4) assistance in finding meaning for life.[16] However, pastoral counselors and psychotherapists often attempt to achieve these goals in different ways.

Characteristics

What are some of the characteristics of relationship? To begin with, much has been written about "the" relationship, while actually each relationship is unique, with the pastoral counselor focusing on its unique characteristics. Thus relationship is not so much a category as a shared experience. Nevertheless, in order to delineate some of the characteristics of relationships, many have studied these relationships quantitatively and have discovered certain trends.

In his analysis of patient-physician relationships in psychotherapy, one psychiatrist saw, fifty years ago, that: "Actually, the doctor-patient relationship is not a tool or instrument of psychotherapy; it is the primary process itself. It is the stage and the play, and not merely the way in which the lines are read."[17]

Certain psychological assumptions play a large part in the characteristics of relationship. These assumptions may be summarized briefly as follows: (1) all conduct has meaning if it is analyzed in depth; (2) people tend to relive early family experiences in all later relationships; and (3) personality growth proceeds through the constructive handling of conflict, not the avoidance of conflict.

Wayne Oates identified four factors that need attention in order to establish a secure counseling relationship. First, the counselor's role must be clearly defined and understood. Second, the frequency and duration of sessions must be agreed upon. Third, a place of privacy must be arranged. And finally, the counselor and client must share responsibly the initiative for setting all this in order.[18]

A review of a number of my more than one thousand case histories based on relationship-focused pastoral counseling experiences suggests that certain trends or stages occur in the relationships. These steps can be delineated as follows:

1. Recognition of problem and request for help
2. Definition of situation and covenant making
3. Removal of threat and free expression of feelings
4. Exploration of negative and positive feelings
5. Mutual understanding and acceptance
6. Clarification of values and goals
7. Externalization and termination of the relationship

The eclectic position in relationship-focused pastoral counseling may be approached consistently from several theoretical systems. Basic to such an approach are the psychoanalytic concepts of personality development and transference, the interpersonal system's theory of human relations, the client-centered emphasis on warmth and acceptance, and the contribution to human understanding made by learning theory. This type of counseling might be described as an eclectic, ego-building, relationship-centered type of pastoral counseling of considerable warmth, encompassing both catharsis and insight and based on the principles of learning theory, the concepts of psychoanalysis, and the techniques of behavior therapy, cognitive therapy, family systems therapy, Gestalt therapy, and transactional analysis.

In the practice of relationship-focused pastoral counseling, the counselor and client engage in the following: clarifying feelings, developing intellectual insight, interpreting, reassuring, questioning, considering past incidents and present problems, and assigning certain thinking, behavior, reading, or writing as homework. The following eclectic methods are suggested:

1. In general, use passive (nondirective) methods whenever possible. Passive techniques are usually the methods of choice in the early stages of therapy to permit emotional release and enable the client to tell his or her story.
2. Use active (directive) methods only with specific indication. In general, therapeutic goals can be achieved with only a minimum of directive interference.
3. Observe the law of parsimony. Do not attempt complicated methods (except with specific indications) until simpler methods have failed.
4. All therapy should be client-centered. This means that the client's interests are the prime consideration.
5. It is desirable to give every client an opportunity to resolve his or her problems nondirectively. When the client does not progress therapeutically in response to nondirective methods alone, it indicates that more directive methods are needed.
6. Directive methods are usually indicated in situational maladjustment where a solution must be achieved with the cooperation of other persons. Some degree of directiveness is inevitable in all counseling, even if only in reaching the decision to use passive or nondirective methods.

Many words have been used in the counseling literature to characterize the therapeutic relationship. A representative sampling might include the following fifteen words: acceptance, confidence, congruence, dialogue, empathy, growth, interest, likableness, limits, mutuality, permissiveness, rapport, respect, sensitivity, and understanding. Brammer and Shostrom propose a continuum as a vehicle for comprehending relationship. For these researchers, relationship was depicted as a balance between (1) uniqueness and commonality; (2) objectivity and subjectivity; (3) cognitive and connotative (feeling); (4) ambiguity and clarity; and (5) responsibility and irresponsibility.[19]

Fiedler's empirical study of the ideal therapeutic relationship is probably more informative in this regard than any other single study. The two extremes that he found are listed below. The statements rated as *most* characteristic of the therapeutic relationship were as follows:

1. An empathic relationship exists.
2. Therapist and patient relate well.
3. Therapist sticks closely to the patient's problems.
4. The patient feels free to say what he or she likes.
5. An atmosphere of mutual trust and confidence exists.
6. Rapport is excellent.
7. The patient assumes an active role.
8. The therapist leaves patient free to make his or her own choices.
9. The therapist accepts all feeling that the patient expresses as completely normal and understandable.
10. A tolerant atmosphere exists.
11. The therapist is understanding.
12. Patient feels most of the time that he or she is truly understood.
13. Therapist is truly able to understand patient.
14. The therapist sincerely tries to understand the patient's feelings.

The statements rated as *least* characteristic of an ideal relationship were these:

1. The therapist is punitive.
2. Therapist makes patient feel rejected.
3. The therapist seems to have no respect for the patient.
4. An impersonal, cold relationship exists.

5. The therapist often puts the patient "in his or her place."
6. The therapist curries favor with the patient.
7. The therapist tries to impress the patient with his or her skill or knowledge.
8. The therapist treats the patient like a child.[20]

On the basis of the data he received when ministers and therapists sorted the same universe of items describing the therapeutic relationship, Becker concluded that pastoral counselors view relationship in essentially the same terms as secular therapists. Pastoral counselors, however, clearly expressed their religious orientation. This underlines the additional, theological characteristic present in pastoral counseling relationships. In these relationships both minister and client are aware of the presence of God and his redemptive power. Ministers convey the acceptance and forgiveness of God in their attitudes and responses to their clients. They recognize moral factors and use spiritual resources.[21]

Functions

Many of the functions of the pastoral counseling relationship resemble functions in the secular therapeutic relationship. One function is to meet the basic interpersonal needs of love, sense of belonging, security, and self-esteem. A lack of these arouses anxiety in a client. The client is able to trust the counselor as these needs begin to be fulfilled within the relationship. Psychotherapist William Schonfield writes that "for every emotionally disturbed person an *irreducible minimum* requirement for successful treatment [is] the provision of a therapeutic relationship with an accepting, understanding, and helping other."[22]

A trusting, therapeutic relationship provides an exceptional setting for interpersonal learning. Clients learn to recognize personal impulses and feelings without becoming defensive or anxious, thereby gaining insight into themselves. In this relationship with their ministers, clients can learn new social skills and new values as well as enlarge personal goals. For instance, a client may need to unlearn or relearn some former ideas about God, ministers, the Bible, the church, or theology.

Another function of the healing relationship is to provide a model with which a client has an opportunity to develop new patterns of response to situations that were formerly traumatic. In the counselor-client relationship, the client reproduces or reactivates his or her characteristic interpersonal behavior, and this provides the arena or proving ground for testing out constructive actions and response patterns. The relationship can then become a pattern or guide in establishing good human relationships outside of therapy.

An immediate function of the counseling relationship is to strengthen the ego, the self, or the conscious will and ideal of a person. In the process, ministers will see in their clients that indecisiveness brings about various forms of defenses and that weakness leads to attempts to escape conflict. The relationship provides the proper situation, attitude, and assistance for trusting oneself to face such things. Thus ministers attempt to communicate the point that God loves all people, thereby freeing clients to choose and respect their choices.

The relationship affords enough support as well as sufficient stimulus, to help clients face themselves and handle the counselor's interpretations and insights. The relationship itself often becomes the topic of conversation in pastoral counseling as ministers seek to help their clients understand themselves or to stimulate them toward insight. For example, I told one client: "I think you do tend to dominate your husband, because you continually try to dominate me by talking on and on even when I try to say something."

Generalization is an overall functional goal in counseling. Clients learn in the counseling relationship to generalize their new modes of behavior to persons outside the counseling setting. Within the relationship, clients learn more appropriate emotional responses, which they in turn externalize into their other relationships. A high school student announced to his pastoral counseling group, "You know, some of the things I've learned in this group have helped me to get along better with the kids at school."

Pastoral counseling, however, retains its distinctively religious orientation, and this fact supersedes the common conceptions regarding the functions of the relationship. Becker said, "The primary religious functions of the pastoral counseling relationship are to bring about an awareness of God's redemptive activity and to communicate acceptance and forgiveness in the relationship which is modeled after the relationship God offers man (sic)."[23]

THE RELATIONSHIP-FOCUSED
PASTORAL COUNSELOR

Much of the quality of the pastoral counseling relationship depends, naturally, on individual ministerial counselors and their skills. Howard Clinebell called ministers "natural relational counselors."[24] The work of counseling is much more than just teaching or using techniques. As a counselor discusses a truth with a client, the truth must be incarnate within the relationship. The life of Christ gave meaning to his words; the same should be true of the relationship-centered pastoral counselor.

Personality

Both the social role and the personality of pastoral counselors attract people who feel that they could discuss their problems with such a counselor. If a kind of analysis could be done on the personality of a pastoral counselor, the following elements might be found: spiritual and physical vitality and strength; neatness and poise; optimism, confidence, and control. In the psychological literature, the traits most commonly mentioned are: (1) motivation for psychological work; (2) good self-adjustment; (3) an orientation toward the needs of clients; (4) good social adjustment; (5) intellectual effectiveness; (6) honesty; and (7) therapeutic competence.[25]

Ministerial counselors should have good self-knowledge. To be effective, they have to have reasonably solved their own problems of living, or at least be sufficiently aware of them to avoid their interference with the ability to listen constructively. The apostle Paul wrote: "My friends, if anyone is detected in a transgression, you who have received the Spirit should restore such a one in a spirit of gentleness. Take care that you yourselves are not tempted" (Gal. 6:1). Most counselors will need to undergo a period of personal counseling themselves to gain this level of self-awareness.

One empirical study found that less well-adjusted and less competent counselors tended to induce clients to model themselves after these counselors. Conversely, clients were found to achieve an adjustment in therapy that was independent of their therapists if the latter were well adjusted and competent.[26] It follows that to be well adjusted, would-be pastoral psychotherapists should have the experience of receiving help as counselees. The American Association of Pastoral Counselors recommends this experience to all its members.[27]

A professional counselor will acquire an understanding of human nature and a mastery of the technical skills of counseling. Yalom, the noted author, states that the maxim " 'It is the relationship that heals,' is the single most important lesson the therapist must learn."[28] Also necessary is a thorough knowledge of human behavior and its physical, social, and psychological determinants. The substantive content of this curriculum should include the following:

- Religious foundations
- Human growth and development
- Social, cultural, ethnic, and gender foundations
- Maladaptive behavior and psychopathology
- Appraisal of individuals and diagnosis
- Marriage and family therapy
- Counseling theories and techniques
- Pastoral counseling theories and techniques
- Group dynamics and counseling
- Substance abuse
- Professional, ethical, and legal responsibilities of the counselor
- Lifestyle and career development
- Research and evaluation
- Practicum and internship

Such knowledge may be accumulated through graduate study, clinical pastoral education, and supervised counseling. Pastoral psychotherapists must master the same sources of knowledge and skill as other psychotherapists. As students of personality they must be as astute as other therapists. This course of study could lead to a master's degree in counseling and, along with adequate supervision and experience, would qualify one for licensing as a professional counselor in most states.

Pastoral counselors are, of course, "persons of God." They identify, without apology, with the Christian community. The purpose of the pastoral counseling relationship is in a general sense sacramental. All pastoral counselors are concerned with discerning reality, even the reality that is beyond this world. They stand for a heritage in which functioning is shaped by theology. They are committed to increasing among all people the love of God and neighbor.

Pastoral counselors need an unusually good ability to relate to people and to discern the elements of the counseling relationship. Carroll Wise stated that the relationship is difficult for many ministers to think about for two reasons: (1) the relationship remains intangible, and (2) thinking about a relationship forces ministers to consider their own feelings and attitudes. Wise also warned that knowing the principles which should govern relationships does not guarantee the ability to create such relationships. One may understand such principles intellectually but find oneself creating entirely different relationships due to an unawareness of the dynamics of one's own personality.[29] Supervision of one's counseling by one qualified to do so usually helps to solve this problem. Edgar N. Jackson states succinctly: "Right relationship within the self is the essential for all other relationships."[30]

A counselor's ability to "live out" relationship principles should be evident in his or her personal life. An experimental study of two psychiatrists working with the same patients revealed that the doctor who established better social relationships with his colleagues and subordinates (described by them as more tolerant, respectful, supportive, and self-confident) also created better therapeutic relationships with his patients than the other doctor.[31]

Counseling ministers also need to have a facility for communication. In his research, Becker arrived at the following conclusions:

1. Communication is a factor of primary importance in the pastoral counseling relationship just as it is in a psychotherapeutic relationship.
2. Communication emerges as the core of the pastoral role in counseling and perhaps of all pastoral work.
3. Communication in pastoral counseling is partly nonverbal, but with slightly more stress on verbal than in psychotherapy.
4. There is somewhat more stress placed on insight in pastoral counseling than in psychotherapy.

5. The adequacy of the communication in pastoral counseling is primarily the responsibility of the pastor himself. He must establish a relationship in which good communication can occur.
6. The content of communication is ideally of a religious nature involving first the conveying of the acceptance and forgiveness of God and the awareness of the presence of God in relationship at a nonverbal as well as verbal level, though other facets of life and experience might be communicated at the same time.[32]

Attitudes

According to Rogers, "the essential qualifications for the counselor lie primarily in the realm of attitudes, emotions, and insight, rather than in the intellect."[33] A number of attitudes are essential for the relationship-centered pastoral counselor. However, these are dealt with at other places in this book and also often enough by other writers that they need only be listed here:

- Empathy (sensitivity to the feelings of others)
- Permissiveness (allowing clients to be themselves and speak their minds)
- Acceptance (unconditional positive regard)
- Flexibility (lack of dependence on a rigid system or technique)
- Spontaneity (immediate expression of real feelings)
- Specificity (using concrete details, not generalizations)
- Confrontation (noting discrepancies between words and behavior)
- Self-disclosure (revealing experiences or feelings similar to a client's)

According to Jerome D. Frank, people do better in therapy when they know they are in therapy, rather than when it is disguised by some other name. They receive more help if their therapists are confident in their abilities and system or technique. They also do better when their therapists are confident of a favorable outcome of therapy and assure them that they can be helped.[34]

Almost all counselors pass value judgments to their clients, expressing favor toward such things as the appropriateness of self-investigation, recognition of feelings, freedom of expression, and personal development. It is unnecessary that the therapist pretend to be an amoral, acultural being without opinions, beliefs, or attitudes.[35] In fact, one psychologist found, contrary to her hypothesis and to her great surprise, that the "amount of client discussion of feelings is greater when the counselor is rated as being more judgmental."[36]

Actually, evaluation may be close to the heart of the therapeutic process, because therapy has taken place when individual clients discover new evaluations of themselves and their world. Unless these clients have the experiences of being judged and yet found acceptable in the relationship, they may wonder if the acceptance is genuine or just a condoning and condescending one.

According to C. W. Brister, ministers, especially those who are pastors of churches, often feel a bipolar tension between the need to be an authority figure, and the necessity to be a flexible person, permitting individuals to grow at their own pace and affirming their own faith under God.[37] Rogers proposes that the "major barrier to mutual interpersonal communication is our very natural tendency to judge . . . the statement of the other person."[38] By contrast, Karl Menninger wrote that "no analyst should pretend that he takes no moral position in regard to what the patient may do."[39]

The relationship-centered pastoral counselor certainly does not want either to exude a condemnatory attitude or to pass judgment prematurely. The counselor should not judge what the client fantasizes about, mentions, or even contemplates. Permissiveness at these times seems to be more helpful to persons seeking solutions to their problems. Emphasis on the current relationship merely indicates that ministers do better to be honest about their real feelings, just as they expect their clients to be. God is the one who actually judges, usually in terms of the natural cause-and-effect processes of life.

Sometimes ministers have such a strong desire to condemn that they cannot wait to see whether the Holy Spirit is already at work in the hearts of individual clients. The process of conviction is the work of the Holy Spirit, not the minister. Divine conviction may take place even when the minister is completely nonjudgmental.

A condensation of Rogers's contemplations about creating a relationship serves as a good concluding summary of the pastoral counselor's part in relationship:

- Can I be perceived by the other person as trustworthy, as dependable or consistent in some deep sense?
- Can I be expressive enough as a person that what I am will be communicated unambiguously?
- Can I let myself experience positive attitudes toward this other person—attitudes of warmth, caring, liking, interest, respect?
- Can I be strong enough as a person to be separate from the other?
- Am I secure enough within myself to permit this separateness?
- Can I let myself enter fully into the world of the client's feelings and personal meanings and see these as he or she does?
- Can I receive the client as he or she is? Can I communicate this attitude?
- Can I act with sufficient sensitivity in the relationship that my behavior will not be perceived as a threat?
- Can I free the client from the threat of external evaluation?
- Can I meet this other individual as a person who is in process of *becoming,* or will I be bound by his or her past and by my past?[40]

THE CLIENT AND THE SETTING

Usually people are not motivated to seek help until external or internal tensions become so great that they swallow pride and determine to act. Often they do not know just what kind of help to seek or which professional person to approach. Almost half of all the people who have sought counseling of any kind have gone first to a member of the clergy.[41] Counselees approach their ministers often in a rather ambiguous manner; they are seeking help but usually have not defined just what ails them. They only know that they are suffering emotional distress.

Physician Martin G. Vorhaus wrote the following:

On any given day somebody—you, I, any one of us—was going along, doing his job, living his life and feeling well. The next day a change began, quickly or gradually, something happened, or an awareness of some modification in doing or feeling became apparent and a metamorphosis took place. A person changed into a patient.[42]

The change involved in becoming a counselee, however, is probably more gradual and less drastic. The inside world of the person gradually became more important than the outside world, and the client has given more and more time and attention to self-exploration regarding emotional difficulties.

Clients who finally present themselves to their ministers have certain needs, such as the need to be dependent, the need for unqualified acceptance and understanding, the need to relieve themselves of painful feelings and ideas, and the need for a cooperative human relationship. Wayne Oates identifies seven different groups of people who come to ministers for counseling: (1) persons with religious doubts and conflicts; (2) persons seeking the forgiveness of God; (3) convalescent psychiatric patients seeking religious dimensions to their cure; (4) persons fearing secular psychotherapists; (5) persons needing psychotherapy but unable to afford it; (6) persons not needing therapy but wanting and needing support; and (7) persons expecting ministers to perform miracles.[43] These people present a great variety of problems to the clergy, including personal problems, marital difficulties, family discord, interpersonal maladjustments, educational perplexities, vocational indecisiveness, psychosomatic disorders, and problems of aging.

Since the amount of time that ministers have to spend in counseling is limited, perhaps a review of the guidelines for selection can assist them in selecting the clients they are most likely to help.

1. Good physical health and adequate intelligence are helpful.
2. Younger people are better because they have made fewer commitments and have fewer crucial decisions behind them.
3. Individuals who are good marital partners or prospects. Married people are better, because in the case of a sexual problem they can practice sexual responses with the full approval of the community.
4. People with a demanding occupation are preferred because they are seriously engaged in life.

5. If the disorder is to be unlearned, it must be a functional one (the product of learning), not an organic disorder.
6. People must be strongly motivated for treatment and cure, because counseling inevitably arouses fear.
7. The more strongly the symptoms have been reinforced, the harder they are to get rid of, hence, the poorer the prognosis.
8. The more personal rewards clients will receive for improvement, the better the prognosis.
9. A certain minimum ability to use and respond to language is necessary, since counseling is carried on by talking.
10. Counseling is more feasible if the clients have had considerable periods of good adjustment rather than a long history of neurosis.
11. Attitudes such as suspiciousness, pride, and passivity interfere with counseling.
12. The need for hospital care or restraint and the potential for suicide must also be considered.[44]

William Snyder, a psychologist who has studied relationship in great depth, concluded that certain traits in counselees aid the establishment of a therapeutic relationship, while others are a hindrance to relationship. He summarized these traits as follows:

> A review of the psychological literature concerning desirable personality traits of clients reveals preference for such traits as tolerance, friendliness, openness, adequate ego strength, personal integration or self-understanding, intellectual adequacy, creativeness, and conscientiousness. Undesirable traits which were listed were hostility or aggressiveness, rebelliousness, anxiety, sexual anxiety, dominance, resistance, evasiveness, dependency, inadequacy, and pathological trends.[45]

Three categories go beyond the scope of the pastoral counseling relationship for obvious reasons. Individuals with the so-called sociopathic personality seek counseling or are forced into it to escape the consequences of their own misbehavior, while inwardly they remain relatively content. The mentally ill should be recognized by pastors and referred to psychiatrists. Those suffering from an organic ailment should be referred to physicians.

Counselees' views of the therapeutic relationship appear to be somewhat different than those of their counselors. "A growing body of research also pays attention to the match between client and psychotherapist, considering such factors as compatibility in terms of background, class, education, and values."[46] While clients may not be conscious of it at the outset, they respond to the attitude of permissiveness. In the counseling relationship they often find they do not need their customary psychological defenses to justify personal behavior. Consequently these clients, sometimes for the first time in their lives, genuinely become themselves. In their relationship with the counselor, they are able to evaluate more accurately their impulses and actions, conflicts and choices, and past patterns and present problems.

These who decide to come to ministers for counseling very likely have basic assumptions about the role of the minister. They presumably think of their ministers as religious persons who are part of a tradition that values individuals and tries to teach them a way of life. Laypeople generally assume that pastors have clear ideas of what is right and wrong. These expectations are important, since "the basis of all successful therapeutic relationships is the patient's faith, or at least hope, that the therapist can help him."[47]

Individual clients perceive ministers according to their past personal experiences. Clinical studies show that clients may view the relationship in one of the following ways:

- *God-follower relationship.* A common type of transference is when the therapist is regarded almost as a god or a god-surrogate.
- *Parent-child relationship.* One client expressed this attitude by saying, "I think of him [the psychiatrist] as a kind father who will guide me wisely and give me comfort when I need it."
- *Teacher-pupil relationship.* Many clients have an exaggerated respect for the wisdom of the counselor and regard him or her as a scholar or teacher.
- *Love-object relationship.* Clients who are starved for affection or sexual outlet may perceive counselors as potential lovers, particularly if the counselors are sufficiently attractive to be suitable objects for affection. Clients' needs may range from a desire for platonic friendship to a frank request for sexual intimacy.

- *Judge-accused relationship.* Clients with guilt feelings tend to project moralism into the counseling situation. The clients assume a defensive reaction, feeling that they are being judged or criticized for their conduct.
- *Policeman-criminal relationship.* Counselors become identified with the forces of the law and are therefore feared. This relationship develops in any situation where the psychologist has had disciplinary functions or is concerned with the administration of regulations.
- *Physician-patient relationship.* Ideally clients perceive counselors as friendly professional people who bring the highest abilities for time and place to the solution of problems.[48]

How a client views the counselor has an impact on the effectiveness of therapy. In one experimental study in which clients saw psychoanalytic, Adlerian, or client-centered therapists, they agreed on the major elements that were helpful in therapy. They indicated that the following aspects of the relationship accounted for the changes that took place in themselves: the trust they felt in the therapist, the understanding of the therapist, and the feeling of independence they had in making choices and decisions. The therapist's procedure that they found most helpful was his or her clarification of feelings which the client had approached hazily and hesitantly.[49]

Clients sometimes drop out of counseling rather suddenly, without prior notice. This usually perplexes their ministers greatly. Some causes for client withdrawal include the following:

- *Relief from symptoms.* Many clients feel that the treatment is successful with symptomatic relief. It is not unusual for clients to telephone after the first interview and state that they feel so well that it will not be necessary to schedule a second visit. Although the clients' problems have not even been touched yet, they do not understand this.
- *Failure of rapport.* Clients may not return if the treatment process becomes too painful before sufficient rapport has developed, or if they never gain enough confidence in the counselor.
- *Crude forms of direction.* In general, clients must make sense of what goes on or they will not develop enough confidence to continue treatment.

- *Improper handling of transference.* Unless the counselor understands the developing transference, it may be mishandled with serious results.
- *Financial problems.* Some clients become so anxious over the mounting costs of treatment that they cannot bear to continue.
- *Uncontrollable environmental factors.* Changes in matters such as employment, school placement, marital situation, or residence may make it difficult or impossible for clients to continue.
- *Resistance.* Clients may withdraw or refuse to cooperate as a manifestation of resistance in order to defend their neurotic way of life. The greatest resistance may develop at crucial points when an important complex is about to be uncovered.[50]

The *setting* where the clients seek help and their knowledge that the counselor is a minister are important factors in the pastoral counseling relationship. Oates has stated that "Christian ministers function in *authoritarian* social settings and *permissive* environments."[51] Ministers and the values they traditionally stand for remain authoritarian, yet their relationship to clients is permissive. Edgar Jackson points out that the "counselee presents himself [or herself], with his [or her] needs for self-acceptance, in an atmosphere that already has established the value of his [or her] being. He [or she] seeks it in a religious community from a pastor who believes in man (sic) in order to help men (sic) believe in themselves."[52]

The church building is often the natural place in which to conduct pastoral counseling. Whether the facility is located in a rural or an urban setting makes a vast difference in the counseling. City pastors' counseling ministries can be sustained by the proximity of professional therapists with whom they can consult or to whom they can refer. Rural pastors, however, are often the only professionally trained persons within miles.

It appears that the use of church buildings as the setting for counseling may only be as old as the modern pastoral counseling movement itself. Historically, ministers counseled church members in their homes during pastoral visits. Currently pastors probably do as much counseling in their own homes and in hospitals as they do in their church buildings. Pastoral psychotherapists usually counsel in pastoral counseling centers, and chaplains counsel in a great variety of institutions [53] as well as in various settings in the military services. What keeps all this counseling "pastoral" is the personal identity of the counselors as clergy, along with their social role, their theological orientation, and their goals in counseling. Hiltner explains:

> There is a sense in which the aims of pastoral counseling are the same as those of the Church itself—bringing people to Christ and the Christian fellowship, aiding them to acknowledge and repent of sin and to accept God's freely offered salvation, helping them to live with themselves and their fellow [humans] in [harmony] and love, enabling them to act with faith and confidence instead of the previous doubt and anxiety, bringing peace where discord reigned before.[54]

In *The Context of Pastoral Counseling,* Hiltner and Colston demonstrated that, when other conditions were approximately equal, people seeking counseling help from a pastor tended to progress slightly further and faster in the same amount of time than did similar people who sought help in a university counseling center.[55] Perhaps the divine presence and the guidance of the Holy Spirit, the favorable expectations of the counselees, and the identity, role, and goals of the Christian worker made the difference.

PART II:
HOW IS RELATIONSHIP USED
IN PASTORAL COUNSELING?

Personality is changed by the therapeutic relationship between the counselor and counselee. A number of counselor activities that promote relationship have been singled out by different writers in the field of psychotherapy. These activities can be adapted to pastoral counseling and thereby can help ministers foster more beneficial counseling relationships with clients.

Otto Rank suggested that counselors do better to concentrate on developing a kind of therapeutic role rather than a technique.[1] Ministers are able, in their role as people of God, to help clients realize their personal worth in God's sight. By becoming aware of the respect, concern, and Christian love that their ministers have for them, many clients come to know something of God's love.

Chapter 3

Initiating the Process
of Counseling

Making and keeping appointments is important to relationship. When pastors arrange for appointments, they imply that there will be unique qualities to this pastoral conversation. It is not unusual for people to raise serious problems for discussion with their pastors upon leaving church after a worship service or in a chance meeting during the week. Pastors, who tactfully remind individuals that serious problems need concentrated consideration, usually are able to arrange an appointment.

The pastor should schedule appointments as soon as possible after the need has been revealed, while clients are highly motivated. When a request comes by telephone, pastors need to discern the degree of urgency or emergency involved. Pastors asked to talk to someone's spouse or family member would be wise to make an appointment to talk first with the person making the request.

The physical arrangements and furnishings of the counseling room can effect the relationship. For example, does the pastor sit behind a desk? Should the pastor display numerous diplomas, licenses, professional books, pictures of the "great," and other trappings that give the counseling setting an authoritarian atmosphere?

Of course, pastors are aware of their position as authority figures in the community; this cannot be denied. In fact, using religious symbols such as the Bible, the cross, or a picture of Jesus can be beneficial in identifying oneself to clients. However authoritative their role, pastors should try to minimize to clients any projection of themselves as authoritarian people.

DEVELOPING RAPPORT

Rapport has been defined as "a condition of mutual understanding and concern about common objectives. The principal purpose of rapport techniques is to build the relationship bridge."[1] When two persons' main concerns and objectives are in accord, they are said to be *en rapport.* Counselors may speak of having good rapport with individual clients when they feel that they have convinced these clients of their goodwill and have earned their confidence. Carroll Wise has written that "a person cannot communicate the deep, intimate aspects of his life to another unless he has a feeling of security, confidence, and trust in the other. This has often been called rapport."[2] However, it is incorrect to assume that rapport can be established easily and early in counseling:

> There seems to be a concept of rapport as "something" that has to be achieved first, at the outset of the counseling process. Consequently, counselors will seek, either deliberately or inadvertently, to invest devices designed to "establish rapport," so that counseling can begin. Rapport is one aspect of the mutuality of the counseling relationship. It evolves from the relationship. *It is not something that can be established first.* [3]

The manner in which pastors socially receive clients when they arrive at the ministerial office has an influence on the rapport in the counseling relationship. In general, clients should receive about the same reception as if invited into the pastor's home. They should be given a genuine welcome and a warm handshake, should be recognized by name, told that they are expected, and invited to be seated and to make themselves comfortable. A greeting may be made by a secretary and then repeated by the pastor. While these things may seem to be insignificant, they are important. For instance, a client once asked me why I so seldom called her by her name.

A pastor must be careful, however, not to overextend the greeting or seek to make it accomplish more than it is intended to do.

> Often a counselee is blocked or discouraged from presenting his difficulties because the counselor prolongs the social reception, interjects irrelevant conversation, attempts to establish

"rapport" with set procedures, reveals immediately some evaluative opinions, reviews his professional qualifications, and frequently interrupts the counselee.[4]

Counseling clergy should bear in mind that crises usually precipitate the first interview and that their clients are likely to experience some degree of anxiety when they first come face to face with their counselors. Few people really want counseling. It is a threatening experience wherein people admit their inability to cope with a life situation. It is a plea for help. Clients may be fearful of encountering social stigma if their friends discover that they are "seeing the pastor." Openly recognizing and discussing situational anxiety by any legitimate means is appropriate and will often do much to alleviate the counselee's discomfort.

Early in the first interview the pastor should discover whether the client came for the interview on personal initiative or at the insistence of a parent, spouse, judge, or church member. Some people visit their ministers at the insistence of someone whose approval they want very badly. With someone who was forced to come, the pastor has the problem of creating an atmosphere in which the reluctant client will experience a personal need for counseling. The coercion involved should be acknowledged. The client needs to be given a chance either to discuss the coercion, if desired, or simply to remain until the time obligation has been fulfilled while the pastor works on other items. Either way, clients will come to understand that their ministers are ready to try to help, but only when the clients themselves are ready to seek help.

According to Rollo May, rapport depends on each person in the counseling situation being at ease. The best way to help put the client at ease is for the counselor to be comfortable and to show it. Counselors should sit comfortably, devoid of nervous mannerisms. In their attitude toward clients, they must balance sensitivity and robustness. Above all, ministers should avoid a stiff, professional manner. This is the chief barrier to establishing rapport.[5]

Legally the pastoral counselor is expected to keep accurate records. In the first several years of my counseling ministry, I was determined not to take notes during interviews; I felt certain that this activity would hinder rapport. Yet as my counseling load increased, writing or dictating process notes between counseling hours or at the end of the day became more burdensome and less accurate. In desperation I began keeping records in the client's presence. I found that counselees rarely had trouble granting me permission to take notes. In fact, the new procedure ensured that I would inform them that I was keeping records and thereby resolved any potential question of ethics. And I found that I actually listened more closely. My note-taking also made obvious to clients that these conversations were a part of our special counseling relationship because no one else ever took notes when they talked. My "charts" were not very well organized until I discovered the problem-oriented record-keeping system. I recommend it to all pastoral counselors.[6] Chapter 11 describes this method of record-keeping.

On rare occasions a client will ask me not to put something on the record for reasons of confidentiality, and it is no problem to honor such a request. If clients become curious about my note-taking, I offer to let them read the notes. Some then get into the habit of reading my notes while we schedule the next appointment. On a rare occasion a client might suggest a correction, usually in reference to some statement of fact.

People coming to pastoral counseling often begin with a "religious" problem. Their initial questions may have reference to the Bible or theology. These questions, though sometimes genuine, are often superficial and are used in an effort to hide deeper and more serious disorders. Such persons, being unsure as to how pastors will respond to their deeper needs, thus pose a so-called religious problem to test the ministerial response before getting to the real issue. As pastors wait and listen with patient understanding, clients usually attempt to present an explanation of deeper problems or confused patterns of living.

PASTORAL APPRAISAL

Among the professions, ministers may have no equal for the variety of human needs they are called on to meet. Therefore, ministers, like physicians, often have the responsibility of performing diagnostic duties.[7] Far too often a pastor has relied on a threefold prescription to solve every problem presented: "read the Bible, pray, and attend church." This regimen has proved helpful to some, but certainly not to all to whom it has been indiscriminately given. In medicine a quack is one who prescribes a cure-all without a diagnosis. This may be said of some pastoral counselors. In a comparative study of the diagnoses reached by a sampling of pastors and psychiatrists in one state, a psychiatrist revealed marked discrepancies between the judgments of the two professions.[8]

Edgar Draper, who has completed training both as a minister and as a psychiatrist, has recommended that pastors use diagnostic procedures.

> Pastoral diagnosis is an orderly, structured approach to pastoral problems which taps all the resources of the minister, including . . . compassion (heart) and . . . objectivity (head). It eventuates in a tentative conclusion as to what the trouble is, opening the way for appropriate action (pastoral treatment). Ideally, the pastor will not be over-influenced by the symptoms (subjective complaints) of [the] parishioner to the exclusion of the signs (objective signals of disturbance). The proposition that proper treatment rests on correct diagnosis should serve the pastor as usefully as the physician.[9]

No matter how accurately done, however, *formal* diagnosis is not always beneficial to the counseling relationship. The compulsive extraction of a case history from the counselee is harmful to the emotional transaction between the counselor and the client. Glen V. Ramsey, who calls himself a "'relationship counselor," explains that diagnosis is an ongoing process that should develop more or less simultaneously with treatment throughout the counseling experience.[10] I prefer the term *pastoral appraisal* to pastoral diagnosis because it avoids medical connotations and transcends some of the misconceptions involved in the controversy about diagnosis in counseling.[11]

Pastoral counselors usually have to make some decisions based on an appraisal of persons who come for help. One such decision relates to referral: "Can I help this person, or should I refer him or her to someone else?" The answer to this question depends partly on whether a psychiatrist or some other professional counselor is nearby, partly on the client's apparent willingness or unwillingness to accept such referral. Yet the more basic question is, "Am I secure enough to discuss this kind of problem, and do I have the ability to help this person find a solution to it?" The minister who counsels must distinguish anew with each client the kind of psychological disturbance presented and its degree of difficulty.

Another diagnostic kind of decision relates directly to the degree of difficulty of the client's problem: "Can I deal adequately with this problem during this interview, or should I schedule another or several more interviews?" The correct answer to this question rests on each pastor's ability to properly evaluate the type of syndrome presented and the degree to which the client is involved in it.

Counselors also try to determine why particular clients have come seeking help at a particular time, rather than the week before, the day before, or even sometime in the future. While I was in resident study, this question so often proved to be revealing that the staff of the social work department at the East Louisiana State Hospital insisted on asking it when interviewing family members who were admitting relatives.

The Bible has traditionally been an aid to pastors as they tended the problem-ridden members of their flock. In a research project at the University of Chicago, Edgar Draper has shown that from religious ideas alone, one may make an accurate personality evaluation and clinical diagnosis. In this study, fifty patients were interviewed in a manner that evoked only religious interests, activities, investments, and beliefs. Each patient was asked to name a favorite or most important Bible character, Scripture verse, and Bible story. All also identified what they believed to be the most religious concept and the worst sin one could commit, along with their ideas about the afterlife and the presence of evil in the world.

The answers to these questions may reveal valuable information about the client, not only religiously, but psychologically. Draper believes that through this study he was able to identify the psychological makeup, character structure, and personality strengths and conflicts of each patient.[12]

Use of the Bible as an instrument of appraisal is only possible in the hands of those with extensive training in personality development and psychopathology. For these people, biblical material in the stream of speech of an emotionally disturbed person may be a means of understanding some of the dynamic causes of the person's distress. Oscar Pfister, in his book *Christianity and Fear,* writes, "Tell me what you find in the Bible, and I will tell you what you are."[13]

Thus the Bible can be a diagnostic tool for appropriately trained ministers in the way that dream symbolism and unconscious communication are to psychoanalysts and that projective tests are to clinical psychologists. With this principle in mind, it is interesting to consider that in some circumstances, the subjective nature of an interpretation of the Bible may reveal something about the personality of the interpreter.

Ministers who counsel should accumulate a working knowledge of personality development and abnormal psychology. Frequent reference to the *Diagnostic and Statistical Manual of Mental Disorders* (DSM-IV)[14] is also important to understand people's problems clearly enough to set the kinds of goals in counseling that are necessary to be genuinely helpful. Forms for use in pastoral appraisal and in connection with DSM-IV are included in Appendixes C and D.

Psychological testing, although it is not infallible, is another aid in appraisal. Carl Rogers points out that the disadvantages of using tests at the outset of counseling are the same as the disadvantages of taking a complete case history. Both imply that counselors will provide solutions to their clients' problems. Such implications are not genuine and do not deeply help clients; instead they tend to make clients either resentful or overdependent. Testing can be used effectively later on in the counseling process, especially when a client requests it.[15]

If at all possible, each pastoral counselor should have obtained answers to at least the following questions by the end of the first interview:

1. *What* is the person's stated problem?
2. *When* did the person first become aware of it?
3. *Where else* has he or she sought help?
4. *Why* did the client finally come to see the minister?
5. *How long* has it been since the person had a medical examination?

6. *Who* can best help this person? Shall I try to help now, or in a series of sessions? Should I refer?

Pastoral appraisal is a means by which a tentative diagnosis may be established. Of course, this appraisal should not be equated with a psychiatric diagnosis, but should be regarded instead as a basis on which the pastor can set realistic counseling goals.

COVENANT MAKING

One task of ministry is to educate clients about the counseling process and method. Counseling literature refers to this explanation process as "structuring" or developing a "contract." Brammer and Shostrom define structuring as "the counselor's definition of the nature, limits, and goals of the general counseling process and the particular relationship at hand."[16] Structuring provides clients with the orientation, framework, and rational plan for counseling.

A certain amount of structure is necessary for responsible pastoral counseling. However, the clergy, traditionally familiar with covenantal relationships such as the Mizpah covenant in Genesis 31:44-53, also recognize the divine presence in human contracts. I like "covenant making" as a more suitable phrase than "structuring" in pastoral counseling, since recognition of the presence of God is one of the unique features of this ministry, which is not connoted in the term "structuring."

Contracts and covenants are different in several other ways. Contracts are external and lean toward legalism; covenants are internal and lean toward grace in the giving of services. Contracts are made to be discharged expediently; covenants promote growth, and nourish rather than limit relationships. Also, the notion of covenant permits ministers to set professional responsibility for one person within social limits. By contrast, the friendship model can imply an exclusive relationship that obscures a person's larger obligations to congregations.[17]

Ministers usually consider covenant making when they recognize the magnitude of a situation, then suggest scheduling counseling appointments. Usually they elaborate on the covenantal relationship during that first interview, especially during the closing minutes when minister and client try to determine a course of action. Discussion of the covenant usually evolves naturally in the conversation, and as a result each person knows his or her respective role and responsibility. This process is similar to informed consent in medical ethics: explaining ahead of time how counseling will proceed.

Determining the interview content is the client's prerogative, while it is the counselor's responsibility to provide an understanding, cooperative climate. The continuation of counseling depends on the client's acceptance and understanding of the structure of this existential encounter. After a comparative study of Sigmund Freud, Karen Horney, Harry Stack Sullivan, and Carl Rogers, a psychologist wrote, "To the extent that the therapist and the therapeutic task and situation are clear and consistent, to that extent the client should progressively respond to the therapist realistically."[18]

As to a second interview, Wayne Oates has argued that the "symbolic act of scheduling a second interview . . . may say to the person many different things: 'I am not too busy to take your problem seriously.' Or it may say, 'I think your problem is serious.' Or it may say, 'I know you came for my "answer," but I am treading water until I can think of one.'"[19] A second interview bonds the counseling covenant and creates a fiduciary relationship.

Certain limits on the counseling situation are inescapable. Perhaps the time limit is paramount. As with other counselors, pastors limit the amount of time given for each interview. Therefore they must explain to their clients at the onset of the interviewing process just how much time is available. Often when time limits are presented, clients hasten to accomplish as much as possible in the time allotted.

Action limits are also required. Counselors should not limit verbal expression, no matter how absurd, unfair, or foolish it might sound. They cannot permit, however, the active expression of certain extremely positive or negative feelings. For example, clients are not allowed to destroy furniture or equipment. They can say that they do not like the counselor, but are not allowed to physically attack him or her. Hurting the counselor would arouse deep guilt and anxiety because the counselor is one of the few people who seems able to help the client.

Limitations of responsibility are necessary as well. Wise pastoral counselors formulate clearly the extent to which they will assume responsibility for the problems and actions of their clients. They make it clear that clients are helped more if each is personally responsible.

Another limitation for relationship-focused pastoral counselors is to protect clients from the emotional overexposure that can result from confessing too much too soon. Clients should feel free to lead the way to the most important and relevant data concerning personal difficulties. It is unwise, however, to reveal hideous sins before the counseling relationship is established. Such confessions seem either to reduce the client's motivation to return, or to make the client feel too much has been revealed and thus he or she feels too guilty to face the minister again.

Conversely, the minister needs to balance the concern for overexposure with a commitment to avoid imposing an extremely narrow structure or directive influence on the counseling situation.

Imposing limits is a part of the continuing process of covenant making, and providing further guidelines at the right time is crucial. This process, as with the entire experience of counseling, is presented to clients as much by demonstration as by explanation, by giving clients the opportunity to participate in a therapeutic experience. Counselors will need to expand the covenant from time to time, in such ways as informing the client of the counselor's need to take and keep notes or recordings; accepting the amount of time needed for the therapeutic proces as well as unexpected delays; understanding the confidential nature of all discussions; setting guidelines for demonstrativeness or physical contacts and gift-giving; and correcting behaviors sush as consistent lateness, broken appointments, and frequent cancellations of appointments.

Chapter 4

Using the Pastoral Role

Charles William Stewart has stated that "the concept of role is central . . . in the counseling relationship itself."[1] A role, as he defines it, "is an *interpersonal relationship within a social system like the family, consisting of an actor or ego, and a social object or alterego.*"[2] On the basis of this definition, I will define *role expectations* as the demands that the actor places on a social object. Role *interactions* are the overt actions of each partner oriented to or affected by the personality of the other partner.

A client's expectations of the pastoral role are often different from the pastor's own conception of it. Since a client probably relates more to the minister in a social role than as a unique personality (especially at first), the pastoral role needs to be considered in a study of relationship-focused pastoral counseling. Initially ministers will usually represent to clients whatever their own religion means to them, which may be quite different from the minister's religion. Yet the psychologically sophisticated minister understands this phenomenon in counseling and accepts it as a fact, though not necessarily agreeing with it.

THE DIMENSIONS OF THE MINISTERIAL ROLE

The ministerial role is multidimensional. This multifarious role is bound up with the breadth and diversity of the tasks performed. The pastoral counselor finds adequacy in the fulfillment of this special role.

Religious Role

Religious counselors have a status and resources that secular counselors do not have. Pastors bring to counseling the dimension of faith and the resources of worship and prayer. They endeavor to reveal a way of life that has cosmic worth and significance. They help people to recognize themselves as beings of worth in the sight of God. C. W. Brister writes:

> The minister's resources include (1) one's identity as God's person and theological education for ministry; (2) the fact that one represents a community of Christian faith, love, and hope; (3) one's authentic, unsentimental interest in the care-seeking person or family unit; (4) therapeutic employment of prayer and the Word of God in relation to the person's concerns; (5) a theodicy of evil and suffering for pastoral practice; and (6) devotion to the eternal kingdom of God beyond the tragic struggles of humankind. A pastor's entire ministry is oriented toward illuminating those values and relationships which shall endure for eternity. (Hebrews 11:27; 12:1—2; 13:14)[3]

Organizational Role

The minister's role is interwoven with the organization—the group of people—known as the church. Ministers represent this institution that has a body of beliefs and practices. Such a position is an asset, because many clients come to ministers unconsciously seeking a group relationship. The church for them may be seen as a security group, a unifying group, or a status group. In association with the institution, each pastor is invested with authority, including the authority to be an interpreter and an adviser.

Often pastors are perceived to be religious and ethical educators—thoughtful, persevering, courageous, and pioneering. As leaders within the Christian fellowship they should be dynamic and prodding, but also understanding and encouraging. They should also be administrators who are firm but selfless, encouraging others to work and to serve others. They are expected to be able to organize with a skill worthy of professional businesspeople and have the wisdom of Solomon and the patience of Job when working out controversies.

Symbolic Role

The symbolic power of the pastoral role provides a strength far beyond that of personal influence, but exactly what form this powerful symbol takes varies from person to person. To the individual struggling to be a responsible person, the pastor is a symbol of responsibility. Another, struggling for maturity, may turn to the minister as a symbol of maturity. In the struggle for a more adequate concept of being, a person may turn to the pastor as a symbol of true being and becoming. To the suffering, the pastor is a symbol of one who cares. Often the minister symbolizes an understanding person with whom one can enter into a close relationship. Pastors may or may not claim any of these symbolic qualities, but they have little control over people's perceptions.

Wayne Oates has pointed out that pastors are considered to be representatives of God, a reminder of Jesus, followers of the leading of the Holy Spirit, and representatives of a specific church.[4] In general, people think that ministers have clear ideas as to what is right or wrong.[5] Ministers are a reminder of childhood training in the ways of doing right, and thus they are a kind of visible embodiment of conscience. By the very nature of preaching, the ministerial role is a judgmental one. However, ministers also remind people of the love of God-in-Christ and the forgiveness God offers. Moreover, the pastor's presence symbolizes a specific congregation of people or, as with chaplains, the invisible church of God.

The Essence of the Role

It is difficult to isolate the essence of the pastoral role, although some have attempted it. Seward Hiltner, for instance, made the following statement:

> As a matter of fact, the minister has one role . . . leader of a particular section of the Christian community. Though [she] has many activities, it is [her] relation to the Christian community which defines [her] role. The role is not only deeper than the activities; the activities would be quite different in their meaning if they were not based on the role.[6]

According to Brister, the pastor's role is that of a "servant to servants."[7] Oates proposes that: "Protestant pastoral counselors . . . will be more in touch with reality by de-emphasizing the father-figure dimension of Catholicism and psychoanalysis."[8]

In spite of these many functions, ministers do not have to be dissociated people in order to maintain the ministerial role. They are people with the character traits and likes and dislikes that make each unique. Ministers need to understand, however, that their popular role-image influences their relationships with people because it is one of the factors already present at the beginning of a pastoral counseling relationship.

DIFFICULTIES WITH THE PASTORAL ROLE

Obviously the pastoral counselor should try to avoid the "ministerial manner," with its sonorous voice, forced sense of humor, back-slapping, and effusive friendliness. Such a "parsonal" approach is the enemy of the personal approach.[9]

One of the very apparent problems attached to the ministerial role and relationship is that people may not confide innermost difficulties to their pastors for fear they will be condemned. Pastors often are referred to (especially in the southern culture) as "preachers." Preachers have had the image of publicly passing judgment and condemnation, and many people fear that they will hear their own stories in the pastor's next sermon. However, wise and ethical pastors disguise illustrations from their counseling *if* used in sermons, or they obtain permission from the client involved before delivering the sermon.

Since many consider ministers authority figures, clients often expect to be given advice and quick solutions for their difficulties. Thus trained pastoral counselors must often teach their clients that a large part of counseling is the process of helping people to help themselves.

Naturally, people outside the church view the minister's role differently from those inside the church. This does not mean, however, that counseling ministers have one stereotyped approach to be used with non-Christians and another to be used with congregation members. Rather, pastors who counsel non-Christians will recognize not only the clients' immediate problems, but also the opportunity to introduce them to Jesus Christ.

AMPLIFYING THE USE
OF THE MINISTERIAL ROLE

Since clients identify ministers with their social role, perceptive pastoral counselors use this role to amplify the therapeutic relationship. Psychiatrist John Levy said that the first step for improving and enriching the feelings which human beings have for each other, and for reducing the dissensions between them, is to clarify the roles that each plays in a given situation.[10]

Along this vein, a minister might say to a client something similar to the following:

> Well, Mr. Anderson, before we start I want to clarify my role with you. You might say that I wear two coats around here— my pastor's coat and my counselor's coat. When I wear my pastor's coat, I represent religion, morals, and ethics, and I speak on these issues publicly. When I see you personally, however, in a relationship such as this, I am wearing my counselor's coat. This means that you can feel free to talk about anything you like and I won't make judgments about you. And I will keep whatever you tell me confidential. Okay?

It is essential that pastoral psychotherapists repeatedly clarify their role in the relationship. One task is to recognize what role clients ascribe to counselors at a particular time: the role of a good or bad parent, spouse, sibling, friend. A basic principle for counselors, according to Alfred Adler, is never to allow clients to impose on counselors a superior role such as teacher, father, or even savior. Such attempts often represent the beginning of a movement on the part of these clients to pull down, in a manner characteristic of them, all persons standing above them.[11]

Ministers who are at peace with the role imposed on them by society learn to be equally comfortable with this role whether in the hospital, the baptistry, the pulpit, the counseling room, or the cemetery. Harry Stack Sullivan wrote that the "person who comes to the interview expecting a certain pattern of events which does not mate-rialize will probably not return."[12] Sullivan felt that psychiatrists should act somewhat the way society expects psychiatrists to act. Similarly, I would say that ministers should demonstrate to clients that they are, in part, the kind of persons they are expected to be.

Like psychiatrists, pastoral counselors must recognize that their skill and training have no therapeutic value unless they are put to use by the clients. In this sense, a pastoral counselor's "expertness" is in divine-human relations, and his or her skill in this regard enables the counselor to lend knowledge and ability to struggling counselees attempting to integrate their divided selves.

Because authority is assigned to the ministerial role by most people, intelligent ministers use this authority appropriately. They acknowledge, for instance, that most people gain status in their own eyes by talking to authority figures. Such persons probably increase their self-esteem even more if the person of authority knows their name, spends considerable time with them, remembers certain things about them, seems genuinely concerned about them, and so forth. These people also esteem themselves more highly if they are able to use the authority's first name and disagree, correct, or express anger toward him or her.

The greatest difficulty with the ministerial role is that it prevents some people from seeking pastoral help. Some are not comfortable with members of the ministerial profession or have no respect for them or confidence in them. More than a few of these individuals eventually cross this barrier once they realize that ministers can provide understanding and acceptance rather than condemnation and judgment. Others never come to that realization.

Chapter 5

Building the Relationship

The counseling relationship, like the more general pastoral relationship, does not spring up instantaneously like the Greek goddess Athena, who sprang full-grown from the head of Zeus. If building a meaningful and helpful relationship for pastoral work requires time, it is even more the case in personal counseling. After a number of interviews, a counselee may say something such as "I couldn't have told you this a month ago, but. . . ." Incapable of being forced, the counseling relationship must be allowed to grow slowly and naturally until it is strong enough to permit such sensitive communications.

According to Carroll Wise, "the relationship is the essential therapeutic element in pastoral counseling."[1] Brammer and Shostrom have said:

> We know of no disagreement to, or contrary evidence on, the assertion that the development of an emotionally warm, permissive, understanding relationship is a first step in the counseling process. The development of such a working relationship characterized by mutual liking, trust, and respect is one of the first tasks of the counselor.[2]

The emotional injuries for which people seek help are often created by faulty relations with significant persons. Only a therapeutic relationship with another significant person can heal these injuries. The "responsibility for creating the ideal pastoral counseling relationship rests with the counselor."[3]

Extensive agreement exists among counselors as to what constitutes a therapeutic relationship. In a good therapeutic relationship, which comprises elements of all other human relationships, the flow of concern is not reciprocal, but is primarily from counselor to client. In psychotherapy there are three dimensions: (1) communication, both verbal and nonverbal; (2) security, including emotional distance between therapist and patient and trust in the therapist; and (3) the status of therapist and patient, which varies between authoritarian, democratic or equalitarian, and passive or laissez-faire.

Pastoral counseling includes an additional dimension—the religious. This dimension includes the awareness of the presence of God, ethics and symbolic values of the pastoral role, the use of spiritual resources, the expression of religious needs, and the counselor's response to these needs.[4]

Counselors need to cultivate the skills required for each of these dimensions of counseling. One counselor training program has a major focus on the therapeutic relationship. Trainees are taught to be empathetic, genuine, and warm through studying tapes of interviews, role-playing, and working with clients under close supervision. All of these exercises are followed by group discussions.[5]

COUNSELOR ATTITUDES
THAT FOSTER RELATIONSHIP

A counselor's emotional activity always has been circumscribed in rather strong terms, and currently, beginners still are warned against certain involvement with their clients. Counselors' feelings are present in most therapeutic relationships, however, and have long since been accepted as a desirable component if they take an appropriate form.

Leona E. Tyler, an experienced social caseworker, worded this principle in the following manner:

> If constructive change of any sort is to occur during the counseling process, it is not enough that the counselor know what [she] is trying to accomplish and use appropriate techniques at each stage. [She] must be willing to . . . become an important part of the client's life—to use the counseling relationship itself as therapy.[6]

Psychologists Bernard G. Berenson, Robert R. Carkhuff, and C. B. Truax, along with their graduate students, have conducted scores of empirical studies on the counseling relationship, mostly at the University of Arkansas.[7] In his book *Relationship Counseling and Psychotherapy,* C. H. Patterson has summarized their findings concerning the "dimensions of response and action in therapeutic conditions." Under the heading of Responsive Dimensions, their findings support their recommendations that the counselor will enhance the relationship by empathic understanding, communication of respect, genuineness, and concreteness or specificity of expression. Under Counselor Action Dimensions, they recommend confrontation, self-disclosure, and immediacy of relationships.[8]

Empathic understanding is an attitude that enhances relationship and is widely recognized and used in pastoral counseling. This attitude enables pastoral counselors to see the world through the client's eyes. "Counselor empathy refers most basically to an appreciative entering into another's ideas and feelings so as to understand the other's world from the other's perspective."[9] People understand themselves better when they are understood by others. Relationship-focused pastoral psychotherapists will try to respond in such a way as to add significantly to the feelings and meaning in their clients' expressions. Counselors do this by conveying the full and deep understanding of the clients at their deepest moments or even accurately expressing feelings beyond the level that clients were able to express themselves.

Such understanding often helps counselees accept personal fears and anxieties, innermost thoughts and feelings, as well as moments of courage, kindness, and love. When clients accept these feelings, they also are better able to understand these feelings themselves and, therefore, are better able to change.

Understanding involves a certain risk. Carl Rogers admits: "If I let myself really understand another person, I might be changed by that understanding. And we all fear change."[10] Thus an insecure minister may have a real problem in trying to genuinely understand another person.

One experimental study showed that the essential ingredient in understanding a client is the counselor's desire to understand. Counseling experts reviewed only the recorded therapist statements taken from interviews. Members of the rating panel had no knowledge of what client statement the therapist was responding to or how the client reacted to the response. Yet the counseling experts could judge the degree of understanding as well from this material as from listening to the entire context. This was rather conclusive evidence that the counselors actually communicated an attitude of wanting to understand, regardless of the content of client statements.[11]

Reverence is another attitude necessary for pastoral counselors in developing good relationships. Other writers discuss a similar attitude under the heading of "respect," but Paul Johnson's term "reverence" is a more appropriate term to use in the context of pastoral counseling.[12]

Ministers rather naturally respect persons, since God has created them. Ideally theirs is a genuine respect, although not necessarily reverence completely free of personal bias. Reverence for clients as God's creatures helps pastors to follow the lead of their clients and move at their pace. Reverence for others enables counselors to respect what life means to these others and to care for them with genuine compassion. This concern permits ministers to let their clients be the persons they are while at the same time expecting and encouraging them to grow.

Before such reverence can develop, pastors must integrate into their own theology a deep conviction that each individual has the right to self-direction and self-determination under God. This form of reverence for their clients helps ministers to maintain confidentiality. Even the counselor's supervision and consultations with professional colleagues, which are needed to serve clients adequately, should only be done with the clients' consent.

The reverence produces an atmosphere in which clients know they are permitted to express their feelings. No attitude should be considered too aggressive, no feeling too guilty or shameful, to bring into the open. Hatred for a parent, feelings of conflict over sexual urges, remorse over past acts, dislike of needing counseling help, antagonism and resentment toward the counselor—all may be expressed. Thus the therapeutic relationship differs markedly from the relationships of ordinary living. The counseling room is a place where clients can bring into the situation, as rapidly as personal inhibitions will allow, all the forbidden impulses and unspoken attitudes that complicate their lives.

James Dittes conducted an interesting experiment in relation to permissiveness. A physiological measure, the psychogalvanic reflex, was used to measure the anxious, threatened, or alerted reactions of clients. During a period of forty-two hours of therapy, patients occasionally felt threatened, even by a warm and gentle therapist, and said such things as, "I think you have to like somebody to communicate. . . . You have to feel free. . . .Who's willing to tell their thoughts to an unfriendly person?" When a client believed the therapist was not permissive, he or she mobilized against threat, even at the physiological level as measured by the psychogalvanic reflex.[13]

Genuineness is the third counselor attitude that helps to create good counseling relationships. Relationship-focused pastoral counselors try to be freely and deeply authentic in a nonexploitative relationship with clients. This attitude is a combination of sincerity, authenticity, trustworthiness, integration, consistency, dependability, transparency, and congruence. Genuineness requires that counseling ministers be aware of their personal feelings insofar as possible, rather than presenting an outward facade of one feeling while actually holding another at a deeper level. Counselors not only need to recognize these feelings, but may also express them through language and behavior. Genuineness does not require that relationship-focused pastoral counselors always express all their feelings; it only requires that whatever they do express is real and not incongruent.

A minister's genuineness helps call forth the reality within counselees. In this way, as they interact in counseling, pastors signify and appropriately express their awareness of the clients' personal experiences. Thus pastoral counselors "ring true" to their counselees. A ring of authenticity held consistently throughout the counseling process often proves to act as a freedom bell signifying that the client is set free to be the person God has created him or her to become.

In addition to the pastoral counselors' awareness of personal feelings and honesty in expressing them, a third quality is necessary for genuineness: consistency. Clients need to be able to count on their counselors to be the same from one interview to the next. Ministers who are consistent in awareness and expression are deemed by their clients to be dependable.

Concreteness, or *specificity,* involves "the fluent, direct and complete expression of specific feelings and experiences."[14] This is the fourth responsive condition of the counselor. It means that the counselor will try to avoid vagueness, ambiguity, and generalization and strive toward differentiation of emotions and behavior.

Concreteness serves three important functions: (1) it keeps counselor responses close to client feelings and experiences; (2) it fosters the counselor's accurate understanding, allowing for early client corrections of misunderstandings; and (3) it encourages the client to attend to specific problem areas.[15] By responding in specific and concrete terms to a client's long, vague ramblings, the pastoral counselor can help him or her sift out the personally significant aspects from the irrelevant material.

TECHNIQUES TO PROMOTE RELATIONSHIP

Techniques are definitely secondary to attitudes. While technique succeeds when attitudes are sound, the reverse is not true. Thus pastoral counselors should try to use only techniques that implement proper counseling attitudes. William and June Snyder noted that the "relationship between therapist and client is as much a part of the essential core of psychotherapy as are the techniques employed."[16] Eugene Kelly stressed, thirty-three years later, that the relationship is more important than techniques.[17]

In a relationship-centered approach to pastoral counseling, counselors must keep in mind two things and apply them to every technique employed: (1) how will this affect the relationship, and (2) will it contribute to the therapeutic objective? These considerations often entail using techniques that emphasize the similarities between counselor and client and de-emphasize the differences. Thus counselors build a stronger relationship as a way of bridging the sense of distance that clients might have felt because of differences they believed to be present.

Counselors may practically demonstrate their attitudes in at least three ways. First, their facial expressions help to convey real interest. More than one sensitive client has detected a counselor's feigned expression of acceptance. Second, the tone and inflection of the voice tells clients something about the counselor's genuineness.

Third, the counselor's posture and physical distance from the client reflect reverence. Usually, if counselors lean toward and sit comfortably close to clients, the latter infer this as a friendly attitude. An attentive posture of "towardness" as opposed to "away-fromness" is important.

Of course, the clients' feelings constitute the guide for all relationship-focused counselors. Besides watching for external manifestations of a client's emotions, counselors also learn to trust their own feelings. They take note of their personal feelings toward the situation and the people whom the clients describe. After analyzing these reactions, counselors can understand their clients' feelings more easily. In regard to a counselor's feelings, Jessie Taft emphasized as long ago as 1933 that "the therapist above all must be able to be what the patient is not for a long time, spontaneous and aware of his own slightest feeling response."[18] This frank, spontaneous revelation of feeling on the part of counselors should, of course, be oriented and reoriented with reference to the ability of individual clients to learn from it.

Conscientious pastoral counselors never promise a solution for client problems or complete relief from symptoms. They only suggest the possibility of such a result. The counselor ascribes to the client any success that comes as a result of their cooperative work. Counselors also modestly disagree with any client inference that they are the last hope for help.

Confrontation can have a valid place in the pastoral counseling relationship.[19] It is one of the counselor's ways of expressing to the client that there are discrepancies in his or her behavior. Robert R. Carkhuff identified three types of discrepancies that call for confrontation: (1) discrepancies between clients' expressions of who they are and who they want to be (real self or self-concept versus ideal self); (2) discrepancies between clients' expressions about themselves (awareness or insight) and their behavior either as the counselor observes it or the counselees report it; and (3) discrepancies between clients' expressed experiences of themselves and the counselor's experiences of the clients.[20]

Confrontation, then, is the pastoral counselor's attempt to bring to the client's awareness the presence of cognitive dissonance or incongruence in his or her feelings, attitudes, beliefs, or behaviors.

In the early sessions of counseling, relationship-focused pastoral counselors are tentative in their confrontations. In later sessions, more direct confrontations may focus specifically on discrepancies. The goal of confrontation is to enable clients to learn to confront themselves and, when desirable, others. "Confrontation of self and others is prerequisite to the healthy individual's encounter with life."[21] Confrontation is not limited to the negative aspects of counselees. It also includes pointing out their resources and assets that are unrecognized or unused.

There are risks in confrontation. It is only useful and effective in relationships that exhibit high levels of empathy and reverence. And, as with genuineness, confrontation can be misused by counselors to vent their aggressiveness, internal anger, or frustration.

For some time, writers have emphasized the counselor's need for *self-disclosure* when working with groups. Self-disclosure is also helpful for the relationship-focused pastoral counselor when working with individuals, couples, or families. The degree of self-disclosure in a relationship may be seen as an index of the closeness within it. Self-disclosure allows counselors to reveal information about themselves—their ideas, feelings, attitudes, and values. They may reveal times when they experienced feelings very similar to or very different from those of their clients.

Ralph Underwood has suggested the following guidelines for "relational confrontation." Pastoral counselors should first disclose how they feel about the relationship before asking, "How do you feel about our relationship?" Second, pastors should be tentative about their perceptions of the relationship. Third, pastors should frame their perceptions in the context of their hopes for the relationship. Fourth, when addressing a problem in a relationship, pastors should acknowledge their own contributions to the situation. Finally, pastors can invite the other person to share feelings and perceptions about what is happening in the relationship.[22]

However, self-disclosure must be for the benefit of the client. It is not done to help the counselor feel better. For this reason, as in the case of genuineness, counselors must think in terms of facilitative or therapeutic self-disclosure. Carkhuff noted that "the dimension of self-disclosure is one facet of genuineness. . . . Spontaneous sharing on the part of both parties is the essence of a genuine relationship."[23]

Physical contact with a client may intensify the positive quality of the relationship, but cautions such as the following have been suggested: "The therapist who has considerable need to touch his patients is revealing a tendency to act out a rather pronounced positive countertransference not unassociated with his own sexual needs."[24] Pastors in Western culture, however, are permitted and even expected to have the personal freedom to touch others appropriately.

For instance, the handshaking ritual carried on at the church door at the conclusion of worship has taken on great significance. In retrospect, perceptive pastors may ask themselves, "Who really touched me?" Jesus, in the midst of the physical contact of a crowd, felt the meaningful touch of the anonymous woman with the issue of blood (Luke 8:43-48). A handshake to begin or end a counseling session is much more widely used by ministers than by any other type of therapist. A minister's hand under the elbow of the bereaved in a gentle lifting motion serves as a physical indication of support. This whole matter of physical contact in pastoral counseling demands further study.[25]

For the relationship-centered pastoral counselor, discussion of the relationship is an essential technique in effective therapy. As I noted previously, priority of relationship is one of the distinctives of relationship counseling.[26] According to William and June Snyder, "where there's a choice of topics, the topic of the relationship is more important."[27]

Immediacy within the relationship refers to the current interaction of the counselor and the client. The notion is similar to the concern with the here and now or the present moment in Gestalt therapy. Carkhuff said, "Usually when the helper cannot express [herself] directly, it is not so much a function . . . inability to express [herself] as it is of the attitudes [she] holds about the helpee in relation to [herself]."[27] It is, of course, impossible for the pastoral counselor to focus continuously on the immediacy of the relationship. It is probably most appropriate to focus on immediacy when therapy seems to be stalled or going nowhere. But it is also useful to look specifically at the relationship when counseling appears to be going well.

Immediacy, while involving the counselor-counselee relationship, is not transference. It involves the counselor as a person, and the real and appropriate feelings that the counselor and the client have earned in their interactions, whereas transference involves feelings from the past.

The pastoral counselor's early attempts at focusing on the relationship are less threatening to the client if they are tentative: "Are you trying to tell me how you feel about me and our relationship?" As their relationship develops, the minister can be more sure of these inferences, and the client more ready to accept them. I have often asked the question, "How are we doing—you and I?"

Counseling is best conducted on the basis of only that information the client reveals to the counselor. Friends and relatives often volunteer to give more information, with the admonition that their names not be mentioned, thus making the information confidential. These situations probably do more harm than good. Once aware of collateral data, a pastor may be inhibited for fear of revealing such to the client. Once collateral data are inadvertently used, clients may become anxious about further undisclosed information their pastors might possess. Collateral data often inhibit counselor honesty and client trust, therefore hindering relationship.

Counselors may study the client's dreams as a way of assessing the relationship. Snyder and Synder noted that dreams reveal much about the character of a counseling relationship. They said that dreams could even be somewhat diagnostic of the relationship, noting that the following types of dreams say a great deal about the relationship: dreams revealing a wish to identify with the therapist; dreams revealing fear or resistance; transference dreams revealing dependency; and sexual dreams associated with the therapist.

The Snyders go on to say that relationship is influenced by the way the therapist deals with dreams in therapy. Their procedure was to elicit from the client all thought associations with, or interpretations of, the content of the dream. Then, through direct questions, they sought secondary associations or explanations of the associations. At this point the Snyders usually presented associations that had occurred to them which they considered the client to be unaware of or repressing. This usually led to further associations, or to discussion along the line of elaboration, acquiescence, interpretation, or denial and resistance.[29]

In my own work with dreams I have often used a Gestalt approach. Believing that each part of the dream belongs to the dreamer and that some elements of the dream may represent unacceptable parts of the self, I ask the client to be or act out each part of the dream. This process usually evokes insight and integration.

In addition to the techniques discussed above, it is helpful to note Lewis Wolberg's rules for the counselor's behavior in building relationships. An abbreviated summary from *The Technique of Psychotherapy* follows:

- Avoid exclamations of surprise.
- Avoid expressions of over-concern.
- Avoid moralistic judgments.
- Avoid being punitive.
- Avoid criticizing the counselee.
- Avoid making false promises.
- Avoid making personal references or boasting.
- Avoid threatening the counselee.
- Avoid burdening the counselee with your own difficulties.
- Avoid displays of impatience.
- Avoid political discussions.
- Avoid arguing with the counselee.
- Avoid ridiculing the counselee.
- Avoid belittling the counselee.
- Avoid blaming the counselee for his or her failures.
- Avoid rejecting the counselee.
- Avoid displays of intolerance.
- Avoid dogmatic utterances.
- Avoid premature deep interpretations.
- Avoid dogmatic analysis of dreams.
- Avoid probing traumatic material when there is great resistance.
- Avoid flattering the counselee.
- Avoid unnecessary reassurance.
- Extend reassurance when truly necessary.
- Express open-mindedness, even toward irrational attitudes.

- Respect the right of the counselee to express different values and preferences from yours.
- Clarify the purpose of the interview as often as necessary.
- Make sympathetic remarks where indicated.[30]

Persons in counseling naturally wonder from time to time about the minister's opinion of them. An occasional word or two of encouragement, perhaps at the conclusion of the interview, will let clients know that their counselor has confidence in them. Such honest expressions do much to enhance the therapeutic relationship.

HINDRANCES TO ESTABLISHING RELATIONSHIP

Skill in cultivating a therapeutic relationship cannot be learned solely by reading books and hearing lectures. Counselors can develop competence in this skill only in actual counseling under the guidance of trained supervisors.

A therapeutic relationship will never arise nonchalantly. Involvement and participation are necessary. Pastoral counselors as well as psychotherapists often feel exhausted after a series of interviews. Maybe tiredness is a necessary correlate to good counseling because something goes out of these counselors and into their clients— something of value, significance, and meaning.

A helping relationship involves a certain amount of mutual fear. Any unknown situation is a source of apprehension, but this feeling is far greater for clients, who have a great deal at stake emotionally and know so little of what to expect from one session to the next. Genuineness is needed to counter this fear. Rogers points out that relationship is constricted if counselors pretend to be something they are not. To act calm and pleasant when actually feeling angry and critical or to pretend to know the answers never helps. Erecting a facade hinders relationship.[31]

A counselor's personality problems may inhibit the therapeutic relationship. For instance, the inability to tolerate hostility—a trait not uncommon among ministers—may make it difficult to develop relationships with clients who display hostility. Personal sexual problems may cause a particular minister to respond with anxiety when the client tells of sexual fears or impulses with which the minister is preoccupied. This may cause the minister to fail to show the necessary warmth, objectivity, and empathy.

A physician has noted other specific counselor personality difficulties that cause "pitfalls in the counseling relationship." Some of these are the need to seek a feeling of importance by rescuing people; the authoritarian personality constellation; an unsatisfied need for love, gratitude, and goodwill; and rivalry and competitiveness with other counselors.[32]

Pastoral psychotherapists can overcome most hindrances to relationship if they make the effort. However, all counselors are limited in the range of individuals they are able to assist. Competent counselors have the ability to recognize the rare person who stands beyond their capabilities and then refer that counselee to another with whom a helping relationship can be developed. As psychiatrist Frank explains, "Whatever other components it may have, the essence of the art seems to be the ability to offer a certain type of relationship."[33]

In spite of writing many positive statements about the importance of the relationship in his earlier works, Carroll Wise alleged in his last book, *Pastoral Psychotherapy,* that focusing exclusively on the relationship "results in the avoidance of process and content, and it tends to place an overemphasis on conscious feeling."[34] I trust that this chapter along with Chapters 8 and 9 will allay any such concern on the part of the reader.

Chapter 6

Observing and Listening

Jesus once said to his disciples: "Many prophets and kings wanted to see what you see but did not see it, and to hear what you hear but did not hear it" (Luke 10:24). Though admittedly taken out of context, these words might also be said of counselors who have developed a heightened perceptiveness.

Physical data are not uniform. A considerable portion of what we seize upon comes through conscious sight, hearing, touch, and smell. A further portion, however, we experience unconsciously. This second portion is more extensive and of far greater importance for psychological comprehension than the first. I will deal with both kinds of data in this chapter.

EYES THAT SEE

One of the pastoral counselor's characteristic marks is sensitivity to people's hopes, fears, and tensions. Pastoral counselors must be particularly sensitive to all the little expressions of character such as posture, facial expression, dress, and the apparently accidental movements of the body. Learn to read character. It is not so simple as reading the proverbial open book; it is more like a traveler going through a strange country and finding everything new and interesting. Everything about people adds brush strokes to the painting of personality portraits. Nothing, not even the smallest movement or change in expression, is meaningless or accidental, for the inner personality continually expresses itself. For example, we lift an eyebrow in disbelief. We rub our noses in puzzlement. We shrug our shoulders in indifference. We wink in intimacy. We tap our fingers in impatience. Or, we slap our forehead in forgetfulness.

Some have objected that there is danger in this kind of reading of other people's character. This objection may be valid if one goes about it like a "peeping Tom." Clinical observation is not for the purpose of setting oneself above another. Conscientious pastoral counselors seek to understand people the better to accept, appreciate, and help them. People prize *this* kind of appraisal, for their self-esteem is elevated as they recognize that their counselors view clients as persons.

For a number of years, psychotherapists offered little for publication about how to interpret body language. They passed this information on to their students by word of mouth. In recent years, however, numerous books for both the professional counselor and the layperson have been published.[1]

The *approach* taken by clients at the initial interview offers the minister a first glimpse into their character. A firm, steady step indicates confidence. A hesitant gait may indicate timidity, betraying the possibility that the person has to renew his or her resolve at each moment. While pastoral counselors should not greet counselees with a lot of social trappings that might be used for meeting aged relatives, they should take a good look at clients at the door and after that maintain good eye contact.

The *handshake* is a symbol of union between people. The *manner* of shaking hands has long been recognized as a significant expression of attitude and character. The "dead fish" handshake is often used by passive people. When the hand is quickly withdrawn, it may indicate that the person is timid and afraid of being hurt. The long, lingering handshake often is used by a dependent individual. The rough, strong handshake, in which a person grips the hands of others like a vice and pumps enthusiastically, may indicate that the person wants to create the impression of a very strong character but, in fact, may feel deeply inferior. By contrast, it is a sign of a healthy personality when the handshake expresses genuine friendliness and interest in the other person.

The significance of *dress* is almost proverbial. Human beings have schooled themselves for many a century in reading the meaning of dress. Clothes do not actually make the person, but details of attire give important hints about the attitudes of the wearer. The disheveled appearance of the mentally ill betrays their lack of concern with the external world and preoccupation with their inner world. Unkemptness may also reveal a lack of self-respect. Contrariwise, exquisite neatness many indicate a rigid and compulsive personality.

Analyzing the meaning of *distance* is another way to understand people. If a client takes a chair near the minister, this implies a friendly attitude; taking a seat farther away indicates fear or the existence of a barrier. Friendliness and interest are normally indicated by movements toward another person; hate and other negative emotions are shown in movements away. The counseling relationship is enhanced when the pastor and counselee are sitting close enough to reach out and touch each other.

Affect is the emotional feeling-tone that accompanies an idea or mental representation. This response is most noticeable in facial expression, although the body often expresses feeling almost as well. Counselors should be able to read people's true joy, pain, or fear expressed in their faces even though they simulate poise and ease. A person's affect may be flat and expressionless, like the so-called poker face, yet this often is an indication of inhibitedness and rigidity toward expressing true emotions. An inappropriate affect signifies a lack of correspondence between feeling and expression. Understanding the affect affords counselors additional insight into their clients' openness to and acceptance of emotions.

Counselors are able to see many signs of *nervousness*. Some of the more obvious include grasping the arms of the chair tightly, wringing hands, biting fingernails, popping knuckles, or crossing and recrossing legs. It is common for counselors observing such to wonder why a client is nervous and what he or she may be struggling with or hiding. However, pastoral counselors must remember that they too are communicating unconscious and nonverbal messages and that clients can intuit much from body language. A forbidding gesture communicates more in a second than many remarks do in an hour. Therefore ministers must always try to be honest about personal feelings toward clients.

Rollo May gave a "general caution for counselors: *hypotheses about an individual's personality pattern are to be made only from a constellation of many different factors.*"[2] No single observation is sufficient basis for a conclusion. In relationship-centered pastoral psychotherapy, keen observations can reveal the significance of the relationship much as a thermometer discloses the temperature. At appropriate times a minister will discuss with clients his observations and interpretations about their unconscious and nonverbal communication. This process usually deepens the relationship between the two.

EARS THAT HEAR

Jesus said, "He who has ears to hear, let him hear" (Mark 4:9). Ministerial counselors have to concentrate more on being listening pastors than talking preachers. Job summarized for his friends the feelings a client might sometimes have: "You are worthless physicians. If you would only keep silent, that would be your wisdom! Hear now my reasoning; and listen to the pleadings of my lips" (Job 13:4-6).

The voice tells much to the careful listener apart from the words spoken. The voice, like good music, expresses a definite mental and spiritual attitude. Yet the particular pitch and timbre, speed and rhythm, volume and pronunciation are not always noticed consciously. These little traits betray a great deal about people.

> Sincerity is shown in a clear voice, courage in a steady one, and an interest in people in a voice that is so distinct that no one can escape contact with it. Certainly the individual who mouths his words or talks so quietly that you must strain to hear him or her does not want to make contact.[3]

Active, accepting, positive listening does not come easily to ministers. It is difficult to maintain this kind of attention toward another. Freud defined it as *gleichschwebend*. The word is onerous to translate because it has both the meaning of revolving or circling and the connotation of equal distribution. The term has been rendered "evenly hovering attention," "poised attention," and "mobile attention," but perhaps most often, "free-floating attention."[4] Successful counselors seek this kind of listening ability.

Wayne Oates has pointed out that listening means essentially three things. First, it means being attentive to what clients are saying. Shuffling papers on the desk, daydreaming, or casting a furtive glance at the clock are all subtle revelations that the counselor is giving only half-hearted attention. Second, listening means letting clients do the talking. Using the active power of silence, which has a way of making small talk transparent, ministers pull clients forward into deeper layers of personal experience. Also, listening means motivating clients to talk. This calls for some positive initiative from counselors.[5]

Listening counselors note how clients express various feelings. As clients experience current feelings, repressed memories return and actively live in the present. Clients may also express ambivalent or opposing feelings about the same object of concern. This is especially true regarding feelings toward God and the church, aggression and passivity, independence and dependence, social approval and rebellion, and self-rejection and self-acceptance.

A word of caution in regard to listening: Skilled counselors may need to take an active approach with some individuals.[6] Oates writes, for example, that some counselors allow depressed persons to talk themselves into greater agitation or depression. If counselors merely listen, clients often conclude that their counselors agree with their self-deprecating statements. This process could even help to precipitate a suicide.[7] Counselors should never tacitly agree that suicide is a good solution to problems. Rather, they should help the client think of reasons why he or she would never attempt suicide.

Pastoral appraisal helps to determine how much listening counselors ought to do with each person. "For the ear tests words as the palate tastes food" (Job 34:3).

In relationship-focused pastoral counseling, counselors should use all they see and hear to make the counseling relationship deeper and more useful. In this process, counselors should mention such observations as soon as it is appropriate. The openness and honesty of the relationship can be enhanced when counselors appropriately confront clients about the things they have perceived and discerned.

Chapter 7

Communication

It is false to assume that communication invariably occurs every time words are spoken. The average person never uses more than a fraction of the approximately 550,000 words in an unabridged English dictionary, yet many of the words that are used have various meanings. With this in mind, it is unlikely that people hearing the words will always think of the same meaning the speaker intended.

It is risky to communicate one's full awareness. Carl Rogers wrote that this choice "determines whether a given relationship becomes more and more mutually therapeutic or whether it leads in a disintegrative direction."[1] Arthur Becker, in his comparative experimental study of the relationships established by pastoral counselors and other therapists, found that there was almost complete agreement between the two groups as to the importance of communication.[2]

Part of the pastoral counselor's covenant with clients has to do with communication and confidentiality. This covenant amounts to more than a promise not to repeat anything the client says, which probably is not a wise thing to promise. Actually clients usually feel free to discuss with others selected tidbits from the counseling sessions, while their counselors are expected not to mention anything. Wayne Oates points out that, in this regard, counseling information usually falls into three different categories, depending on the degree of threat of exposure inherent in the information.

First, Oates says, some information discussed is community knowledge, already known by many people. Second, other information is privileged communication that the pastor could pass on in specific instances if the client gives permission. For example, the responsible pastoral counselor regularly collaborates with other professionals. Supervision and case conferences among professionals also fall into this category. Third, some communication is strictly confidential information. This is information, usually of a confessional nature, that the minister receives as unto God. This is passed on to no one.[3]

REFLECTIVE COMMUNICATION

Reflection of feeling is defined as the "attempt by the counselor to express in *fresh* words, the essential attitudes (not so much the content) expressed by the client."[4] In reflective communication, ministers can help individuals (1) to feel deeply understood; (2) to infer that feelings motivate behavior; (3) to realize that they are responsible for evaluating themselves; (4) to recognize their own powers of choice; (5) to clarify their thinking, thus seeing their situation more objectively; (6) to know that their counselors have not regarded them as unusual and different; and (7) to examine their deeper motives. An illustrated summary of several types of reflection are presented below.

Content

While content responses prove that the counselor has heard the client, it is considered an error in counseling to reflect content continually. Using this method, counselors only "parrot" client statements in essentially the same words. This puzzles clients and does not convey understanding. An example of this is the following conversation:

>   Counselee: I've always considered becoming a preacher because that's what my mother always wanted me to be.

>   Minister: You've always sort of considered becoming a preacher, because that's what your mother always wanted you to be.

Such an approach may leave a bewildered client wondering, "Isn't that what I said?" Or, "What's wrong with the way I said it?"

A pastoral counselor attempting to be reflective might have responded:

> Minister: You just went along with her since you never thought of disagreeing with her?

This response would help to get below the surface and to touch the undercurrent of feeling that the client expressed.

Depth

Relationship-centered counselors try to respond in such a way as to match the depth of client statements. They respond to the clients' underlying feelings that produced their words. Some ministers are consistently too shallow in their reflections:

> Counselee: It's not that I don't like you, pastor, but I dread coming here to talk to you.

> Minister: You like me all right, but you dread our talks.

Other ministers are too deep and interpretative:

> Minister: Because you like me, you have dreaded our talks because of what could possibly happen between a man and a woman.

A client would probably meet this response with denial or a change of subject. Perhaps a more accurate response is:

> Minister: You like me all right, but you dread your feelings which accompany our talks.

Meaning

Relational counselors try to avoid adding to or taking from the meaning of a client's statements. Thus they do not supply words, complete thoughts and sentences, nor do they respond only to the last thing said. For example:

Wife: I can't trust my husband, even though he says he loves me.

Husband: I do love you.

Minister: You see, he says he loves you.

This minister has "watered down" the meaning of what the couple expressed. In the following statements the minister has assumed too much:

Minister: You won't trust your husband no matter what he says.

Accurate reflection of the client's meaning may appear to be easy, but too often the ministerial counselor responds from a personal perspective rather than from the perspective of the client.

Language

Ministers should try to use the language most appropriate to individual clients in order to enhance their relationship. Whether counseling an illiterate homeless person or an educated professional, the pastoral counselor must develop the ability to use the other person's language. By tuning in to the client's expressive frequency, the minister can communicate understanding in the client's language:

Student: Pastor, is it all right for a Christian to "make out" with his girlfriend—you know, kiss her a lot?

Minister: You're worried about whether or not Christian young people ought to "make out."

Occasionally a counselor may need to help the client to label a feeling:

Counselee: I guess I felt like Dad didn't like me or wished I was different or something. I can't quite put the feeling into words.

> Minister: Could we say that you feel as if your father *rejected* you?

Delayed Reflection

Once a subject has been introduced into the dialogue, it is fair game for discussion. Counselors might not catch the first mention of an emotionally charged subject, or they might recognize such an area but decide to wait until a more appropriate time to deal with the subject. For instance:

> Chaplain: Mrs. Marshall, when we visited before your surgery, I believe you said that your husband had died just a year ago.

SILENCE AND PAUSES

Silence or pauses in conversation present a problem to many beginning pastoral counselors. Often they create anxiety for both counselor and client, thus disturbing the counseling process. After reading hundreds of verbatim accounts of interviews, I have concluded that many inappropriate pauses, occurring when the minister obviously should have spoken, could have been avoided if the minister had simply listened to the client and reflected back what was said.

Silence is always used for a purpose, however, whether or not its meaning is ever discovered. First, silence can be of two types: positive and accepting, or negative and rejecting (such as the "silent treatment"). Second, a pause may mean that the client is deciding which of several things to discuss next. Typically there is a silent moment before getting down to serious work. A third meaning of silence is that of hostile resistance or anxious embarrassment, especially if a particular client was sent by someone else. Fourth, a long pause may be a signal that a client is struggling with a painful or vague feeling too elusive to put into words easily. Fifth, a pause might be labeled as "anticipatory," because the client is expecting some reassurance, information, or interpretation from the counselor. Sixth, a client might simply be thinking over what has just been said, and to speak at that moment might destroy a fruitful trend of thought associations. Finally, a client might pause to recover from the fatigue of previous emotional expression.

Appropriate pauses by counselors are valuable to relationships. The pastoral psychotherapist's silence forces many clients to talk. Being in the presence of another silent person often moves client attention to the task at hand—personal problems. Research with projective psychological tests has indicated that introversive persons are often deeply creative individuals with rich inner lives. Many taciturn clients discover that even though quiet, they are liked by their patient pastoral counselors. When ministers remain silent after a significant expression of feeling, clients, having been granted time to think, sometimes bring forth profound insight. A counselor's silence can also slow the pace of interviews when necessary.

C. W. Brister summarized the variety of counselor comments and found that dialogue in pastoral counseling is dynamic and responsive rather than static or passive. Ideally, when counselors comment, their words are chosen with deliberate care, with one of various purposes in mind. Counselor comments may express *empathy* when seeking to identify with the client, *invite* the client's self-disclosure, *reflect* the client's feelings back for thought or clarification, *affirm* what has been said, help to *effect transitions* from one pattern or thought to another, and, occasionally, *confront* the person with Christian truth or with possible consequences of the feelings or plan of action. Also, the counselor is free to *summarize* what has been said so that a plateau may be achieved in the conversation. Counselors may comment to *reassure* or offer support when in keeping with the reality of the situation. However, some counselors err by reassuring sufferers prematurely, prior to the dawning of an inner pathway of light.[5]

The words of Jesus in Matthew 10:19-20, even though taken out of context, are still appropriate to the communication of pastoral counselors: "Do not worry about how you are to speak or what you are to say; for what you are to say will be given to you at that time; for it is not you who speaks, but the Spirit of your Father speaking through you."

Chapter 8

Dealing with Negative
and Positive Feelings

Members of the clergy do not always recognize and deal with their parishioners' and counselees' inappropriate positive or strongly negative feelings or actions. Many ministers hope that if ignored and denied, these influences will just go away.

But clients *will* maneuver to obstruct counseling, and ministers *will* need to take appropriate action. These maneuvers by clients are referred to collectively as "resistance." Two opposing forces skirmish in clients: the motivation to improve the life situation, and the tendency to maintain life patterns that have at least brought them thus far. The term "resistance" is used by psychoanalysts to indicate the "instinctive opposition displayed toward any attempt to lay bare the unconscious."[1] The biblical phrase closest to resistance is "hardening the heart."

THE DIMENSIONS OF NEGATIVE FEELINGS

Clients display negative feelings when they perceive their counselor, the topic of discussion, or the situation as threatening. A client's anxiety is aroused in response to the threat, and the client defends himself or herself against the anxiety through behavior that is negative in nature.

A principal value of negativism (all types of negative feelings) for counselors is its indication of general progress and its use as the basis for further appraisal. When counselors note negative symptoms, they take the first step toward appropriately dealing with them by ignoring, reducing, or using them. Negativism gives counselors an opportunity to glimpse into their client's defensive structure. This procedure helps informed pastoral counselors determine whether their clients are ready to explore certain feelings at that time. Another benefit of negativism is that it protects clients from the disintegration of personal defensive structures prior to the establishment of new constructive behaviors.

Some negative forces are consciously held in the mind, some are subconscious but retrievable to conscious thinking, and some are unconscious and only accessible through dreams, hypnotism, symbolism, and other indirect means. To avoid confusion, I use these terms in this book: *negative feelings*, referring to conscious attitudes; *defensiveness*, implying subconscious emotions; and *negative transference*, relating to unconscious forces.

Negative Feelings

Often clients have certain negative feelings about counseling that date to the time of their first inclination toward seeking an interview with the pastor. Clients usually express these attitudes quite early, perhaps when arranging the appointment or early in the first interview. Negative feelings will recur, for they are never settled "once and for all." Such conscious negative reactions as the following are included in this category: wondering if "just talking" can really help, contemplating the pastor's ability to help, debunking counseling, and being hostile about another's insistence that the client seek counseling.

When relationship-focused pastoral counselors recognize negative feelings, they try to bring into expression hostile attitudes clients may have toward themselves, employers, parents, teachers, rivals, the counselor, or even God. Too often ministers spring to the defense of those impugned. Yet, even in this area counselors are most effective by helping clients express their real feelings without taking sides. If counselors are able to assist clients in facing these feelings openly, recognizing them for what they are, and admitting them as their personal feelings, then clients are often more comfortable with discovering positive qualities in themselves.

In the first interview with one client who had been a drill instructor in the Marines, he told me that he finally had to leave the military

because his superiors wanted him to "counsel" with the boys sometimes instead of yelling at them. I told this ex-Marine that I didn't
think he really believed in counseling and had only come because
his wife had insisted that he learn to control his temper. After revealing that counseling was not exactly his idea, the client said that, on
the contrary, he did believe counseling could help and that in fact he
had majored in psychology in college after leaving the Marines.

Defensiveness

Defensiveness is the subconscious thwarting of the counseling
process. One sign of defensiveness is the client's overdependence
on the counselor. Such a client may continually seek advice, extra
appointments, telephone counsel, or prolonged sessions. A client
may try to dominate or be dominated by demanding authoritative
answers, complimenting or criticizing, and refusing to talk spontaneously. Other types of defensiveness include:

- Intensifying symptoms or a flight into health
- Intellectualizing the discussion of feelings
- Talking superficially or discussing less significant topics
- Forcing the counselor to take the lead
- Being late, leaving early, or missing appointments
- Showing competitiveness with the counselor
- Rejecting interpretations by the counselor
- Forgetting topics previously discussed
- Inquiring into the counselor's life or feelings
- Not fulfilling assigned tasks between counseling hours
- Terminating counseling too soon

When defensiveness appears in the context of the discussion,
relationship-centered pastoral psychotherapists meet it as forth-
rightly as possible. Once these defenses have been fully expressed
by a client, they tend to dissipate and may never reappear. Listening
and understanding does not always resolve every defense, however,
because these negative symptoms are deep-seated and disguised.

Attempts to unravel defensiveness may take any of these forms:
(1) calling the client's attention to the defense and exploring its

manifestations; (2) pointing out possible reasons for the defense; (3) reassuring the client in a tangential way about the matter being defended; or (4) diverting the conversation temporarily to a less threatening matter.

In dealing with broken appointments, Carl Rogers noted two important steps in the process. First, the counselor should scrutinize the last interview for coercion, rejection, or growth. If one of these is present, it may account for the missed appointment. Second, the counselor should help the client feel perfectly free to return or not to return, perhaps by a letter.[2]

Negative Transference

A client who remains in the process of pastoral counseling over a period of several months will probably exhibit negative transference at one time or another. Freud called this the most powerful resistance to treatment.[3] In negative transference, the client presents negative symptoms by perceiving the counselor as similar to an unloving, rejecting, or fearsome person from the client's past life. Counselees often display such strong emotions as fear, hate, and hostility.

Negative transference comes from the unconscious mind, and although it is difficult to recognize and resolve, pastoral counselors will encounter it and should learn to recognize it. The prescription for resolving negative transference is to bring these feelings and behaviors into each client's conscious understanding. Counselors may do this by inquiring into prior arousal of these feelings and by asking about people in the past for whom the counselor might serve as a reminder.

Negativism of one form or another often presents itself in the process of counseling. Unless the counselor recognizes and deals with this negativism properly, a client may terminate the relationship too soon while the counselor wonders why.

A DESCRIPTION OF POSITIVE FEELINGS

Pastoral counselors generally do not have much trouble dealing with positive feelings in counseling. These feelings are not as personally threatening as negative feelings, although in their more extreme forms they are a problem. Pastors are customarily liked and prefer this reaction to dislike. Difficulties arise only when they are liked too well and too intimately.

Positive Feelings

Strictly speaking, a client's conscious positive feelings do not hinder the counseling relationship. Rather, they promote it. In this sense they are not a resistive force in counseling. Since in their more extreme form they do thwart the therapeutic progress, however, these feelings are usually considered along with the sidetracking phenomenon called *positive transference*. Yet even Freud noted the difference between the two types of feelings: "Positive transference is then further divisible into transference of friendly or affectionate feelings which are admissible to consciousness and transference or prolongations of those feelings into the unconscious."[4] The following chapter discusses the concept of transference in greater detail.

Jesus accepted love as the dominant motivation in mature living. Love means an attitude that places the interest and welfare of other people on a level equal to that of oneself. The capacity to give and accept love in both its sexual and nonsexual meanings is essential to the integration and growth of the personality. Gradually, as clients learn to accept a kind of nonthreatening affection that does not demand mutual satisfaction from them, they come to the place where they can express a similar attitude toward themselves and other people. Insofar as this kind of love is expressed in the counseling relationship and accepted by counselees, this love becomes a potent curative factor in personality.

A client sometimes becomes emotionally involved with the pastoral counselor because the counselor usually behaves somewhat differently in the consultation room than elsewhere. Clients often falsely assume that their ministers would show the same level of attention and understanding in a typical human encounter that they show in the office. Furthermore, for many clients the relationship with their pastoral counselors is the best they have ever had. The positive feelings that clients have for their ministers as persons and as professional helpers enable the former to accept suggestions or interpretations and to comprehend the counseling process in a most cooperative way.

Three experimental studies provide further insight into positive feelings. The first analyzed whether different types of therapists have different types of patients who tend to remain in treatment or break off prematurely. If so, what characteristics of therapists might be responsible for the differences in their patients' reactions to them? Among other things, this study found that "therapists rated as most warm and friendly were able to keep in treatment a larger percentage of unproductive patients than therapists rated as least warm and friendly."[5]

In another study, two psychologists attempted to determine the extent to which client dependence and therapist expectation of client improvement could be considered relationship-maintaining variables in the psychotherapeutic interaction. The results indicated a strong positive relation to client pretherapy attraction to the therapist. Also, the psychologists obtained partial support for the hypothesis that favorable therapist expectation of client improvement could function to maintain the therapeutic relationship.[6]

The third study investigated the ratability of client likability and the relationship of this to success in psychotherapy. The more successful clients were liked better than the less successful clients to a degree that was statistically significant.[7]

Thus, there is a wide range of expression of positive feelings. Some of the manifestations include (1) a feeling of comfort in the counselor's presence, (2) attraction to the counselor, (3) therapist optimism toward counselor improvement, and (4) client likability by the counselor.

Positive feelings seldom threaten the counseling relationship. For the most part these feelings are dealt with normally and naturally. When relationship-focused pastoral counselors recognize these feelings, they reflect them back to their clients, reassuring them of the value of these feelings in counseling and of the importance of not being afraid of such feelings.

Positive Transference

Counseling pastors do not have to deal with extreme positive transference very often. One reason is that this tends to occur more frequently in long-term therapy. Since pastors engage primarily in short-term counseling with a view to the present and the future, transference-love, which is linked to a client's past, does not often occur. This reaction, however, can be quite threatening to ministers when it appears and, when not understood, can be devastating to the counseling relationship and to the minister's personal life or career.

Positive transference occurring between a counselor and a client of the opposite gender is "an inordinate unloading of emotional regard of the patient on to the analyst, and [is] indistinguishable from falling in love with him [or her]."[8] Clients of the opposite gender speak of "love," which they expect to have returned. This change in behavior often occurs at a time when counselors are trying to help clients remember a particularly distressing and heavily repressed piece of personal history. Clients frequently lose all interest in treatment and declare they are well. Such transference-love is a resistance that hinders continuation of treatment.[9]

When pastoral psychotherapists are confronted with transference-love in counseling, they should not spurn or repulse it out of fear, but most resolutely withhold equal response. This phenomenon usually requires supervision or consultation. Freud suggested that such love should be recognized and treated as unreal—a feeling that could be traced back to unconscious origins. This reaction from counselors helps their clients to feel safe enough to allow the causes of transference-love and all the fantasies arising from sexual desires to come to light. Counselors should stress the unmistakable element of resistance in this "love." Genuine love would make these clients intent on involvement in treatment so as to gain status in their counselors' eyes through recovery. When these clients use this transference-love to thwart and resist treatment, however, they may become more interested in their counselors than in dealing with the symptoms that have made their lives miserable.[10]

The relationship-focused pastoral therapist gives due respect to this phenomenon, recognizing the subtle hints of positive transference in extended counseling situations and helping clients to feel free to discuss these feelings. Counselors serve as symbols, and clients' feelings can be directed to anyone sitting in the counselor's chair. Bearing this in mind should help counselors not to attribute the professed love of a counselee to their own good looks and winning personality. Consult Chapters 9 and 13 for further discussion of this topic.

Chapter 9

Handling Transference and Countertransference

Transference and countertransference are almost always present at some level in counseling. Relationship-focused counseling must challenge the assumption that clients deal only with conscious material while psychiatrists, psychoanalysts, and psychotherapists deal with unconscious material. Too often counselors are presumptuous about their ability to differentiate between the two in the counseling process. The greater the number of hours logged in a one-to-one situation, regardless of the counselor's professional identity, the greater the probability that transference and countertransference will occur.

TRANSFERENCE

Transference has been defined as a "psychological bond between people in which one person's reaction in a current relationship is influenced by his [or her] former relationship patterns to significant persons rather than by the stimuli present in the context of the current relationship."[1]

This reaction is limited to the unrealistic, inappropriate, unearned roles or identities unconsciously ascribed to the counselor. Usually occurring in association with regression, transference presents new interpersonal manifestations of old internal conflicts. The concepts of resistance, displacement, and projection are also used in reference to transference.

The major significance of transference is the insight it gives into client feelings and behavior toward persons important to them outside of counseling. If clients can be helped to see how their reactions to their counselors are caused by a confusion of those counselors with other persons, the inappropriateness of similar reactions outside of counseling becomes more obvious. If a client projects the childhood image of a father or mother onto the counselor, for example, the client may be doing the same to other individuals, such as professors or employers.

Transference serves many other important purposes in counseling. Through transference, clients are able to express distorted feelings without the usual defensive responses. The counselor's adept handling of transference responses gives the client confidence and thereby supports the rational relationship. This increases the momentum of the process as well as the likelihood that the client will remain in counseling until a successful conclusion can be reached. Through the counseling process, insight into the origin and significance of transference feelings come to light. Such feelings were born through poor interpersonal contacts and are resolved through a corrective interpersonal experience in counseling. Open discussion of transference phenomena serves as an excellent means of enabling clients to understand themselves.[2]

Transference is an illegitimate and irrational appropriation of old feelings to new people. Just what is transferred from the past to the present? The basic drives of love and hate, attitudes, defenses, and any mechanism that clients use to defend themselves against anxiety stirred up by repressed impulses.

When clients express irrational feelings of transference toward their counselors, knowledgeable counselors inquire into the possibility that such feelings have a history. "Have you ever felt this way before toward any other person?" is a typical question counselors ask these clients.

Undue personal dependence on counselors is very likely the most difficult problem connected with transference. Dependent clients insist that their counselors take over their decisions and self-management. Because such attitudes usually show up early, counselors need to take this opportunity to discern whether they have the ability to cope with the alternating apathy and aggression that often accompany dependency. When these clients do not obtain the solutions and support they seek, the resulting aggression often severely tests the counselors' abilities to control their own negative feelings and to maintain an attitude of acceptance and understanding. Dependence on treatment is realistic; dependence on the persons doing the counseling, however, is unrealistic.

Labeling all client feelings for counselors as transference is an easy and false way for counselors to protect themselves. Because of the natural focus by therapists on transference, some use the term to include all that goes into the relationship between counselor and client. This is to misuse the term. Ronald Lee and others have used the term "working alliance" to refer to the "relatively nonneurotic rational rapport the client has with the pastoral therapist."[3] The rational responses of the client toward the counselor's personality refer to the relationship. One sign of a counselor's self-confidence and maturity is the ability to acknowledge when a client's perceptions are correct and to accept as genuine those feelings based on correct perceptions.

DEALING WITH TRANSFERENCE

Having dealt with transference in more general terms, we must now study more closely this phenomenon in pastoral counseling. Edgar Draper has written that the "subject of transference in pastoral care is worthy of a book in itself."[4]

There are people who, having had no previous contact with the minister, develop an immediate and intense transference reaction at the first meeting. In general, though, psychologically mature persons are less likely to experience overwhelming transference reactions immediately.

Carl Rogers believes the "possibility of effective brief psychotherapy seems to hinge on the possibility of therapy without the transference."[5] Pastoral counselors do well to note this probability. Rogers admitted that some transference reactions (usually mild, but occasionally strong) appear in client-centered therapy, but he maintained that these reactions do not expand into a transference neurosis. The reason for this is that in Rogerian therapy, therapist response to transference is the same as to any other client attitude: therapists try to understand and accept. Acceptance then leads to the recognition by clients that these feelings are within themselves and not in their therapists.[6]

In addition to *simple acceptance,* a number of other responses for working through and preventing a deep transference are helpful. The relationship counselor asks *clarifying questions* regarding the forms of anxiety which the client seems to be manifesting. The transference feeling in the client's statement calls for counselor *reflection.* The minister may give direct *interpretation* of the transference feelings. Focusing on *what is occurring rather than why it occurs* provides a more fruitful technique for handling difficult transference problems. In general, counselors *call attention only to negative transference feelings* because focusing on transference causes clients to react in the opposite manner. As a result, counselors do not call attention to positive transference unless it reaches a level where it interferes with therapy. Pastors should always consult their supervisors when transference becomes unmanageable. Finally, counselors may *refer* clients to therapists qualified to give more extensive psychotherapy if situations develop to an intensity that is beyond the competence of the minister.

Lester Bellwood, in his research on "transference phenomena in pastoral work," came to the following conclusions: (1) well-adjusted pastors may recognize irrational elements in another's reactions and may tactfully point them out without knowing anything concerning the dynamics of transference and countertransference; (2) the pastor's spouse also needs to be a rather well-adjusted person, for as a team they are in the position of being viewed as surrogate parents by members of the congregation, and possible objects of transference reactions; (3) pastors should understand the dynamics of transference in order to serve their congregations more effectively; (4) pastors are in a good position to provide supportive therapy, for they carry the message of unconditional love. Their natural role is that of maintaining a positive relationship, and they have a better chance of maintaining the positive response if they quickly recognize transference reactions and immediately bring a parishioner back to reality; (5) pastors who carry the message of the unconditional love of God and maintain a positive relationship with their parishioners are in a position to take the additional step of transferring the dependency needs of parishioners to the church and to God; and finally, (6) since transference and countertransference responses may carry both positive and negative implications, and the way in which they are handled in either case may determine the degree of their constructive or destructive results, seminary training should attend to these specific phenomena.[7]

Although it provides insight into the client, transference is not relationship. Relationship has to do with the real, rational, appropriate, and earned interactions within the counseling situation. If pastoral counselors present themselves as genuine persons in counseling and act accordingly, they are usually able to focus on relationship in counseling rather than worry about uncontrollable transference. Learning to manage transference should be done under the supervision of a highly trained and experienced pastoral psychotherapist. It is helpful for counselors and supervisors to listen to tape recordings of counseling sessions or to have their supervisors, with counselees' permission, observe the counseling situation through a one-way glass window.

COUNTERTRANSFERENCE

The situation is reversed in the case of countertransference, which has been defined as follows: "When the second person's reaction to the first person in the same relationship is also influenced by his [or her] former relationship patterns to significant persons rather than by the stimuli in the presence context, he [or she] is involved in countertransference."[8]

Many psychologists maintain the important point that *not all therapist affect is countertransference.* However, there is strong adherence to the psychoanalytic Law of Talion: that every transference situation is answered by a countertransference.[9]

Because it is an unconscious phenomenon, countertransference is difficult for therapists to detect. A number of writers have listed signs of countertransference. The following is a combined list of attitudes or feelings the therapist may experience in the case of countertransference:

- Anticipating or dreading a counseling hour
- Being bored, drowsy, or inattentive during therapy

- Overidentifying with a client
- Resenting or feeling jealous toward a client
- Feeling personal pleasure, disgust, or depression as a result of the counseling hour
- Fearing a client
- Being impressed by or disliking a client
- Protecting or punishing a client
- Rejecting or becoming angry with a client
- Feeling parental fondness for a client
- Fantasizing about or being preoccupied with a client
- Dreaming about a client
- Feeling strongly positive or negative toward a client
- Touching or patting a client inappropriately
- Feeling an intermittent sense of frustration or annoyance
- Experiencing extra-therapy difficulties with a client
- Being anxious during a counseling hour
- Responding with love or hate toward a client
- Being careless in arrangements: forgetting or arriving early or late for appointments, or extending them needlessly
- Cultivating a client's dependency
- Arguing with a client or becoming defensive
- Consistently reflecting or interpreting too soon or incorrectly
- Regretting or wishing for the end of therapy

Only since World War II has much been written on the subject of countertransference. Until then the subject was rather embarrassingly neglected. Freud first wrote about the phenomenon in 1910, but he considered it a therapeutic error to be avoided. For social workers such as Jessie Taft, psychiatrists such as Frederick Allen, psychologists such as Carl Rogers, and many neo-analysts, however, a positive warmth toward clients was considered a strong therapeutic agent and highly desirable. Counseling seems more and more to be perceived not as something that happens to one person under the observing eye and occasional help of another person, but as a two-party transactional relationship. William and June Snyder conclude that "there is much support, then, for the existence and desirability of some expression of countertransference in good psychotherapy."[10]

My study gives strong indication that something of the counselor's real and conscious feelings ought to be allowed to emerge in the interaction of counseling. These feelings, of course, would be the counselor's investment in the relationship, *not* countertransference. Judd Marmer proposed in 1955 that much semantic confusion could have been avoided if the term "countertransference" had always been used only to refer to the irrational aspects of the patient-physician relationship, and if different terms had been used for its rational aspects.[11] Perhaps thinking of the concept of relationship as the rational, real, and conscious aspect of the counseling interaction is helpful at this point.

Unlike therapists of some persuasions, William Snyder not only saw no objection to admitting positive affect for clients during therapy, but believed that this procedure truly helped to build a more positive relationship. He thought that when counselors felt friendly, they should reveal the fact and that this gesture would seem to contribute to the goal of a better and more therapeutic relationship.[12]

Almost everything written or implied in this section concerning counselors equally applies to ministers who counsel. Ministers do well to concentrate on relationship; countertransference is best avoided where possible. Once pastoral counselors are able to recognize countertransference with some accuracy, however, they need not fear it.

Chapter 10

The Use of Christian Resources

A relationship-focused pastoral counselor brings to counseling a familiarity with, and understanding of, the resources of the Christian faith. Using these resources is as normal for a minister as breathing, since they contain the minister's view of life and are often assimilated into his or her very character. Three of these resources have been selected for discussion: confession and forgiveness, prayer, and Scripture.

CONFESSION AND FORGIVENESS

Confession is a part of the Christian tradition. In confession, a person verbalizes to another the evil he or she believes resides within and thereby places it in the external world. Otto Rank wrote that "verbalization, which constitutes the only emotional expression in the therapeutic situation, is not only a symbolic substitute for action or emotion but also actually represents a rejection (putting out) of parts of the ego."[1]

Protestants, particularly in the free church tradition, tend to minimize the importance of confessing their faults one to another. No matter what their tradition, however, pastoral counselors do not fulfill their role until they help clients to face guilty feelings honestly and to find divine forgiveness. In the trusting counseling relationship, clients often find that they can confess sins and honestly confront feelings as never before. In the midst of a meaningful relationship with pastoral counselors, clients begin to build or rebuild a relationship with God.

Ministers must consider several facts in the practice of hearing confessions in counseling. First, isolation and alienation are the main effects of a known transgression. Individuals who know they have sinned are unable to face their community as they did before. Therefore confession is more than mere catharsis; it is the process of making social what had been otherwise an isolated experience. Second, ministerial counselors are wise not to accept too quickly that the confessed sin is the most troublesome one. Clients often run a "test case" first to get a reaction. Third, it is a hazard to take the admission of a fault too lightly and to reassure the person too soon, so that the client is made to feel guilty over having felt guilty.[2]

In the counseling process the client usually becomes aware of the presence of God and of the redemptive process. Good pastoral psychotherapists convey the acceptance and forgiveness of God in both their attitudes and their responses to the clients, thereby using spiritual resources to meet specific needs of a client. Where clients have known only guilt, betrayal, and shame, the minister tries to help them realize self-understanding, trust, and divine forgiveness.

Access to the forgiveness of God is undoubtedly the most unique characteristic of ministerial counseling. People who really believe that God has forgiven them have the burden of guilt lifted and the fear at the heart of guilt extinguished. God's forgiveness was described by the English clergyman Leslie Weatherhead, not as the cancellation of all the effects of sin, but as the restoration of a relationship. Forgiveness means that the relationship with God continues as though a sin was never committed. It means the ending of the penalty of sin; there is no longer any separation from God. Forgiveness arrests the progressive deterioration of character. The consequences of sin in life do remain but usually are given a more understandable personal interpretation.[3]

Of course, ministers themselves are not able to forgive, but they are able to stand or kneel alongside the penitent and pray for God's forgiveness. By such action ministers indicate that they too are sinners who stand in need of God's grace and that the channels of forgiveness are open to them both if they honestly and humbly call on God.

Carroll Wise has suggested that pastoral counseling should not limit this resource by only talking about it but should actually put the attitude of forgiveness into practice. Basic to the experience of forgiveness is the experience of being accepted. As the counselor accepts anything that the client communicates, regardless of the depth of the guilt involved, the counselor breaks through the deep feelings of isolation that guilt always produces and ushers that person into a relationship in which he or she is again accepted. Pastoral counseling may not seek to bring a sense of forgiveness in one overpowering experience, but may seek to help the individual work out the attitudes that are creating guilt. It seeks to help a client accept forgiveness by removing that which makes accepting it difficult.[4]

To define the content of the divine-human encounter as the communication of grace or the forgiveness of sin is one thing. To prepare the way for such an encounter is quite another matter. Knowing the ultimate word in theological terms does not equip pastoral counselors to communicate it effectively in existential relationships. Preparing the way for the communication of divine grace is an extremely complex task, deserving of the utmost in professional competence and religious commitment.[5]

After persons experience God's forgiveness, they usually begin to reconsider all the other relationships in their lives. Clients who have faced their own humanity and have been accepted and forgiven by God are more permissive with those about them. Even though others commit grievous errors, clients are often able to reassess their relationships and to become more forgiving toward them. At this stage clients may discuss with their pastoral counselor various things they could do to make restitution.

PRAYER

In counseling, a distinction needs to be made between formally spoken prayer and the deeper meaning of prayer as a reaching out of the mind for understanding and help. Wayne Oates differentiates this way: "Pastoral counseling, when properly understood and practiced, is in and of itself a total experience of prayer."[6] Where one person seeks to know the truth about himself or herself through the assistance of another, there is prayer. In expressing a need, like an infant crying out for help, there is prayer. As people go through pain and suffering within the counseling relationship in an effort to find themselves, there is prayer.

Such prayer requires communication between client and counselor. However, both ministers and clients tend to feel a sense of isolation at the beginning of each counseling session. The Holy Spirit, recognized as the Third Presence, breaks down the wall of partition that causes both parties to feel alone and enables them to enter an interpersonal relationship. Thus the Holy Spirit helps create their communion.

One of the basic values emphasized by discoveries in the field of psychotherapy is the indispensable nature of insight, or inner revelation, to the wholeness of personality. Prayer is often thought of as begging God for gifts or confessing to God what has already been decided to be sin. These concepts of prayer, however valid, tend to seal off such insight. In the more legalistic frames of reference, prayer becomes almost a self-flagellation or a self-exaltation experience. In the more liturgical frames of reference, prayer often becomes a set pattern crowding out the creativity and spontaneity of the Holy Spirit within. However, an evaluation of the prayers of the Bible reveals that the persons who prayed them expressed their frankest feelings to God. In doing so they learned to understand these feelings themselves.

Relationship-focused counselors encourage clients to pour out their souls before the Lord. Ministers often become a sort of third person in such a process. This prayer is not a formal "bowed head" prayer, but one in which persons express to their ministers the sense of injustice that they feel toward God for the frustration they must bear. The Almighty has been able to tolerate this sort of prayer throughout history; ministers, however, are often quite disturbed by it. They sometimes rush to God's defense, as did Job's counselors, by becoming argumentative, talkative, and coercive. Yet when these pastoral counselors discover that God accepts their real selves, they no longer need to protect God against the real self of anyone else.[7]

Occasionally prayer is misused by pastoral counselors. Some naively suggest prayer as an easy solution to problems. Prayer may be offered as a substitute for personal insight, and many people feel they should say in a prayer what *ought* to be said, rather than expressing their real feelings. Dependent persons who expect God to give a ready-made answer may demand that the pastor pray for them. The pastor may find that he or she must require these persons to stand on their own two feet before God and to do their own praying. The pastor should do so gently, but with a trusting confidence and firmness that lets such people know that the counselor is not a crutch. The pastor should not let chronically dependent persons use prayer as a sedative, an opiate, or a placebo. Prayer is a way of life, not an addiction whereby to avoid life.

SCRIPTURE

The Bible states that "whatever was written in former days was written for our instruction, so that by steadfastness and by the encouragement of the scriptures we might have hope" (Rom. 15:4). Donald Capps, professor of pastoral therapy at Princeton, reviewed the Bible's role in counseling and found that beginning with Wayne Oates in 1953,[8] the Bible has been widely used by pastoral counselors to comfort, instruct, or diagnose.[9]

There can be no doubt that ministers will apply the truths and doctrines of the Bible in counseling as they personally understand it and as it applies to particular situations. This is not the same however, as quoting Scripture or telling Bible stories. When the minister is dealing with a client who is familiar with the Bible, Scripture becomes an available resource to a degree that is impossible without that background.[10]

Using the Bible in counseling often injects the dimension of authoritarianism into the counselor-client relationship. If ministers are concerned about maintaining a permissive relationship, they find that the frequent use of scripture creates tension by introducing the element of threat into the context of counseling. As a symbol of authority, the Bible is sometimes used as both a sword and a shield by ministers. It easily becomes an instrument whereby ministers express hostility, or a means of protection when they themselves feel threatened.

By contrast, William E. Hulme illustrates how the Bible can be used constructively in counseling situations. After the client has related an insight, the pastor, instead of restating that insight, may on occasion correlate the insight with a reference from the Bible. If the client appears to show a genuine interest in the correlation, the pastor may write the reference on a card at the close of the session.

Pastors must restrain themselves from overdoing this kind of biblical correlation or it will give the impression of preaching.[11]

Giving clients pertinent selections of Scripture to think about as homework might be called "bibliotherapy." Using the Bible for homework extends the counseling relationship into the period of time between counseling sessions. Bibliotherapy is a timesaving feature in counseling when it is used to start clients thinking about related features of their feelings. Clients can be stimulated in their thinking as the Holy Spirit stimulates their apperception of the Word's message. Bibliotherapy also enables the client to find support through Scripture between the periods of counseling.

Not all people counseled by ministers are open to bibliotherapy. Determining when to use Scripture depends as much on the client as on the nature of the problem. Unless the person is receptive to bibliotherapy, assigning such homework is more harmful than beneficial.

It is possible that the client who approaches the minister with feelings of anger because the Bible and prayer have not produced magical solutions to problems may *only* come to understand and feel their relevance through the counseling relationship. Through this, such a person may be able to come back into a devotional fellowship with God.

Chapter 11

Utilizing Problem-Oriented Records

The problem-oriented medical record as developed by Lawrence L. Weed, MD, has come to be more and more widely (although not uniformly) used in medicine.[1] It is a logical and systematic method to document the findings and conceptions about the diagnosis and treatment of the patient. The problem-oriented record (POR or Problem-Oriented Medical record—POMR) consists of four major components: (1) the establishment of a database, which includes identification, chief complaint, present illness, medical history, social history, family and marital history, and mental status; (2) the collection of all problems into a numbered problem list; (3) the formulation of plans for each problem, including collection of further data, treatment, and education of the patient; and (4) the follow-up of each problem summarized in the numbered progress notes.

The traditional psychiatric record has been obviously lacking in consistent organization, clarity, accuracy, and readability. Thus in psychiatry, interest in the POR has increased noticeably in the past several years.[2] Even though the formulation of problems has proved to be particularly vexing and the detail and time-consuming aspects of the system have been criticized, acceptance of the POR has continued to spread.[3]

For the pastoral counselor, a knowledge of the POR is important for several reasons. The POR serves as (1) an adjunct to the memory of the counselor about the history, observations, and past and present treatment of a counselee; (2) a readily accessible repository of up-to-

---

An earlier version of this chapter was previously printed as "The Problem-Oriented Record in Pastoral Counseling," by Richard Dayringer, in *Journal of Religion and Health (17)*1: 39-47, 1978.

date information about the counselee; (3) an accurate reflection of what is actually taking place in treatment; (4) a record of the development and testing of clinical hypotheses; (5) a source of information for research purposes; (6) a scientific document available for the scrutiny of supervisors or peers for teaching purposes; and (7) an accurate legal document.

Pastoral counselors have, I am afraid, been rather lax in the keeping of good records of their work with people. In our history of pastoral care, Richard Cabot, MD, was quite impressed that Russell Dicks kept records of his prayers with patients and felt so strongly that such a minister should be brought on the staff of the hospital that he paid him out of his own pocket. I wonder if we pastoral counselors have hidden behind "confidentiality" at times as an excuse for not keeping good, professional records. With the advent of managed care and the demand of third-party payers for treatment plans, professional, pastoral psychotherapists need to become quite familiar with the treatment plan approach to therapy.[4]

DATABASE

By defining the collection of information about the counselee as data, the POR helps to avoid interpretations based on incomplete information. Data are collected as much as possible without evaluation. This is to minimize the temptation, once a diagnostic hunch occurs, to gather further data in support of that impression to the neglect of other important material. This helps to avoid a kind of "tunnel vision" and the overlooking of important areas. The POR stresses separating (1) the collection of information about the counselee from (2) the integrative process of problem definition and from (3) the formulation of treatment approaches.

The intake process will often take the pastoral therapist more than one interviewing hour. It may take an hour and a half or two hours in a single session or two or more hour-long sessions to collect the database using the following outline. The data are gathered from the counselee's discussion of his or her problems, not in a question-answer fashion.

1. *Identification:* List name, birth date, sex, race, marital status, source of referral, address, phone, source of information, and reliability.
2. *Chief Complaint:* Write a brief statement, preferably in the counselee's own words, explaining why the counselee came or was brought for counseling.
3. *Present Illness:* The major objectives here are to (1) define problem areas in the person's, couple's, or family's life, and (2) gain adequate information for diagnostic formulation. This may be written in a narrative style or the problem title style, using the initial problem list as the format. For each problem a statement about the time and type of onset, characteristics of the problem, precipitating factors, and the counselee's emotional responses should be included.
4. *Medical History:* Include current and past medical history of significance to the present illness; be sure to get the name, address, and phone number of the counselee's physician. When was the last consultation or physical examination? Include any problems with appetite, weight, or sleep.
5. *Social History:*
   - *Economic:* Include sources and level of income, indebtedness, who handles finances and how, and feelings about economic status.
   - *Occupational and Military:* Outline job and military history, job security, reasons for job changes, relationships with authority, peers, subordinates.
   - *Educational:* Record level and type of education; family educational norms, relationships with teachers and students, feelings about school.
   - *Recreation and Hobbies:* Does use of leisure time include people, things, or solitude?
   - *Religion:* Include affiliations, training, level of current practice, role or influence of religion in current life.
   - *Sexual:* Assess sexual information, experience, functioning, and feelings.
   - *Medications and Drugs:* Include alcohol, tranquilizers, antidepressants, illegal drugs, prescription medicine, and sedatives.

- *Interpersonal Relationships:* Evaluate quantity and quality of friendships.
- *Legal:* Current and past interaction with legal authorities.
- *Cultural:* If counselee belongs to a cultural subgroup, how does this affect choices of behavior, treatment, or attitude? Include length of time in city of residence, city of birth or hometown.

6. *Family and Marital History:*
- *Family of Origin:* What kind of persons were father, mother, siblings, and how did patient relate to each? Position in birth order.
- *Marriage or Cohabitation:* Describe spouse or partner, give history of relationship, and assess interaction between the two including control, affection, assertiveness, satisfaction, and recreation.
- *Family of Progeny:* Describe children or others living in the home, including counselee's interaction with them in regard to love, anger, discipline, or disagreement; assess satisfaction with living situation.

7. *Mental Status Exam*:
- *Attitude and Behavior:* Include appearance, clothing, grooming, facial expression, attitude, motor activity, mannerisms, anxiety.
- *Mental Activity:* Describe spontaneity, relevance, responsiveness, coherence, thought associations, discontinuities, blocking, distractibility, flight of ideas.
- *Mood and Affect:* List range of affective expression, consistency, appropriateness.
- *Thought Content:* Assess relevance, completeness, abstractness, unusual or bizarre occurrences, hallucinations, delusions, obsessions, referential, congruence.
- *Sensorium and Intellect:* Consider orientation, attention, memory, recall, calculation, reading, writing, comprehension, concept formation, knowledge.
- *Insight and Judgment:* Record awareness of dysfunction, choices of behavior, ability to achieve satisfaction.

8. *Psychological Testing:* Include summary of findings.
9. *Diagnostic Impression:* Interpret according to standard nomenclature (DSM IV).

The database can be accumulated by note-taking during the sessions or dictated after the first or second interview. I find that it flows smoothly and does not take too long, never more than thirty minutes. Sections that cannot be completed are noted "Information incomplete" and serve as a reminder to gather date data later.

PROBLEM LIST

After collection of the database, the Weed system stresses the formulation of a problem list that summarizes "*all* the patient's problems, past as well as present, social and psychiatric, as well as medical."[5] Each problem should be listed at a level of refinement consistent with the pastoral counselor's understanding of it but avoiding diagnostic guesses. Of course, the minister will sometimes have personal problems in dealing with a particular counselee, but they should not be listed. The question, "Is this a problem for the counselee?" should always be answered in the affirmative before a problem is defined. The problem list can run the gamut from specific behavioral description to broad diagnostic categories. As Weed has emphasized, the problem list "is a 'table of contents' and an 'index' combined, and the care with which it is constructed determines the quality of the whole record."[6]

The problem list is dynamic in the sense that each problem is dated at the time it is defined, new problems are added as defined, current problems are amalgamated and further refined, and old problems become inactive or resolved. The date of onset of a problem can be added in parentheses if that is known. Differentiation of those problems agreed upon by the counselee from those he or she does not understand or agree with but that seem clear to the counselor seems to be important. I agree with the opinion that counselees put forth greater effort toward solving those problems with which they are in agreement.[7] Thus, reviewing the problem list with the counselee solidifies the working covenant and enlarges the counselee's informed consent.

The problem list naturally follows from information collected in the database. Some examples from my own counseling records will illustrate the method:

Patient A. B. 31-Year-Old Single Male

Problem Number	Date Defined	Active Problems	Date Inactive	Date Resolved
1	9-22-96	Religious doubt		10-28-96
2	9-22-96	Job problem		
3	9-22-96	Broke up with girlfriend		
4	9-22-96	Depression		
	9-22-96	A. Terminal sleep disturbance	11-24-96	
	9-22-96	B. Poor appetite	11-24-96	
	9-22-96	C. Lack of energy		
	9-22-96	D. Weight loss		11-24-96

Problems should be listed separately unless there is a clear relationship to another problem. If two problems are clearly related but require separate treatment programs, they should be listed separately. This can be done in two ways. The main problem may be entered with subcategories specifying the various manifestations of the problem as in problem number 4 with patient A. B. above. Or the problems may be listed independently, but their relationship to other problems may be indicated by the use of "secondary to" (2°). Thus, patient A. B.'s problem list could be written as follows:

4 Depression
5 Terminal sleep disturbance 2° to 4
6 Poor appetite 2° to 4
7 Lack of energy 2° to 4
8 Weight loss 2° to 4

INITIAL PLANS FOR EACH PROBLEM

A clear statement of each of the counselee's problems at the counselor's level of understanding leads to Weed's next step of a treatment plan for each problem. Weed has designated three areas into which plans for each problem should be subdivided.

The first of these is *collection of further data*. This may include gathering more information from the counselee or family, obtaining old records from a previous therapist, or performing psychological testing.

Couple C. and D. E., Ages 41 and 46

Problem Number	Date Defined	Active Problems	Date Inactive	Date Resolved
1	10-1-96	Communication problem	12-8-96	
2	10-1-96	Anger	11-26-96	
3	10-1-96	Resentment and suspicion (Dorothy)		
4	10-1-96	Low self-esteem (Dorothy)	11-12-96	
5	10-1-96	"Bitching" (Clark)		
6	10-1-96	Listening (Clark doesn't feel Dorothy listens when he talks)		
7	10-1-96	Infrequent coitus		
8	10-1-96	Drinking problem (Clark)		
9	10-9-96	Too much time alone (Dorothy)		
10	10-9-96	Resistance to change (Clark)		10-14-96

The second category is *treatment plans*. Special plans for dealing with each problem, such as a description of a behavior modification program or an explanation of the type of psychotherapy to be used, are included here.

The third area of emphasis is *counselee education*. Here notes are recorded about what specifically *will* or *will not* be told the counselee about his/her problem, treatment, or outside information that the counselor may have.

Family F, G, H, I, J, and K. L., Ages 40,38,18,14,9, and 4

Problem Number	Date Defined	Active Problems	Date Inactive	Date Resolved
1	7-18-96	Wife's uncontrolled expression of anger (yelling and spanking)		
2	7-18-96	Wife's fantasies and accusations that husband is unfaithful		
3	7-18-96	Wife's occasional, visual hallucination (date onset 5-1-95)	5-28-96	
4	7-18-96	Wife's depression		
5	7-18-96	Which church to attend		9-9-96
6	7-18-96	Social isolation	11-3-96	
7	7-18-96	Incomplete database		8-21-96
8	8-11-96	Husband's withdrawal		
9	8-21-96	Harry's mental retardation		
10	8-21-96	Harry's anger		
11	8-21-96	Jeff's enuresis		

An illustration of how this works comes from the L family, whose problems are listed above. To address problem number 11, Jeff's enuresis, the plan is as follows:

1. Gather more data. Check with Dr. Gress to see if there is any medical or physiological reason for the enuresis.
2. Treatment. (a) Use insight-oriented therapy with Jeff to see how he understands the causes or benefits of his enuresis. (b) Have him and his parents make a urination frequency graph, charting daily whether he wets the bed.
3. Counselee education. Instruct his parents, especially his mother, not to supply him with dry pajamas and bedding in the middle of the night. Also, stop his intake of liquids by 7 p.m.

PROGRESS NOTES

The fourth basic element in the POR is systematic recording of follow-up notes on each of the problems delineated in the problem list as they are dealt with session by session. Each progress note is numbered and dated. Problems that emerge for discussion during the session are listed according to their original title and number, and the interaction is summarized. Notes can be made during or following the session as the counselor prefers.

A format is suggested by Weed for this summary. *Subjective* data include important symptomatic reporting of the counselee about the problem. Statements by the counselee about his feelings, mood, activities, plans, evaluation of counseling, and progress or statements by family or friends are recorded here. Quotations are often used.

Objective data include observations by the counselor or other health professionals about the counselee. This will contain such information as appearance, behavior, and affect. The results of testing could also be included here.

The *assessment* section is the place for the counselor's analysis of the problem. It should summarize his or her current understanding of the problem and should attempt to answer such questions as: (1) Why is this a problem for this counselee at this time? (2) How does the problem disrupt the functioning of the counselee? (3) What needs to change and how can the change be effected? (4) How is this problem related to the counselee's other problems? (5) How did the counselee come to have this problem?

The *plans* section is used for revising initial plans. The first letters of the four words, subjective, objective, assessment, and plans, form an acronym, SOAP. So, all progress notes are "soaped" in this system. An example of this from the E couple, whose problems are listed above, follows:

Progress notes: C. and D. E., 10-9-96

Problem 2: Anger
- S: He likes to swear loudly to blow off steam. She dislikes this behavior and often leaves the room when he does it.
- O: She did not exhibit any anger in the session. He often sounded hostile.
- A: She internalizes her anger. He doesn't use his constructively.
- P: Insight therapy and Bach's Anger Museum.

Problem 4: Low self-esteem (Dorothy)
- S: She feels self-conscious about her body and thinks she is ugly. She doesn't like her husband to admire other attractive women.
- O: She was very neatly dressed in clothes usually worn by younger women.
- A: Low self-esteem.
- P: Insight therapy.

Problem 7: Sex Problems
- S: Dorothy likes to snuggle and talk before intercourse. He doesn't talk much when they're in bed because he doesn't want to; nor does he think he's very good at "sweet nothings."
- O: She likes to touch and talk romantically. He gave her a good compliment about her sexual responsiveness.
- A: She's probably not sure he still loves her. And in light of Problem number 4, she needs reassurance that she pleases him.

P: Insight therapy and Masters' and Johnson's techniques for impotence.

Problem 9: Too much time alone (Dorothy)

S: Clark said he thought Dorothy was at home alone too much. Dorothy agreed but claimed her hip problem has prevented her from doing some things she used to do.

O: She was rather passive and somewhat satisfied with her current state of existence.

A: Lack of involvement. She is overly dependent on him.

P: To discuss her participation in some activity, especially something they can do together.

Problem 10: Resistance to change (Clark)

S: Clark stated that he was satisfied with himself and didn't feel he was willing to or needed to change.

O: He presented this as being a problem.

A: He is denying his part in the marital problem.

P: Insight therapy.

Organization of progress notes according to the POR continually reminds pastoral counselors to think systematically about their counselees and provides evidence of whether they have actually done so.

CONCLUSION

The records that pastoral therapists keep on file are a commentary on the adequacy of the counseling done. For some counselors, records are an indictment of their work because the file folders are either almost empty or their contents look like an unassembled jigsaw puzzle. The POR offers an organizational scheme for fitting the pieces of the puzzle together meaningfully as they are located. PORs are subject to the same abuses of sloppiness and shortcuts as other record systems, although these deficiencies are more immediately obvious.

The record is a vehicle for communication with oneself or with others, where appropriate, for referral, research, or supervision. As a message to pastoral counselors, the POR serves primarily as a mechanism for the retention of information. Reviewing the POR often discloses inconsistencies, omissions, and inaccuracies in problem descriptions and interventions.

As a source of information to be passed on to another therapist (with the counselee's permission) in cases of referral, the POR can be readily understood. It also provides the pastoral counselor with a dignified legal document if he or she should ever be hauled into court.

The POR gives enough organization to counseling notes to create a methodology for research. All sorts of factors can be selected from an accumulation of such records for evaluation, statistical analysis, or review.

The POR is unsurpassed as a teaching tool in supervision of counseling. The supervisor can easily sample the student's understanding of such problems and readily provide positive reinforcement for the student's good work, identify omitted problems, demonstrate intercorrelations between problems, suggest alternative treatment approaches, and closely monitor the follow-up.

The best thing of all about the use of the POR is that it seems to improve the treatment and care of the people who come for help.

Chapter 12

Closing and Termination

All things must come to an end. Each counseling interview must close (closing), and each series of counseling interviews must terminate (termination). The time limits of the therapeutic situation, as with the other limitations, furnishes the counseling relationship with many aspects of the life situation. The appropriate closing of each interview and the termination of the counseling situation are both important to the therapeutic relationship.

CLOSING THE COUNSELING SESSION

The recognition of mutual time limitations usually has an early spot on the agenda of even a first interview. If both minister and client decide that a number of interviews will probably be necessary to deal responsibly with the problem at hand, then the length of each interview is normally a part of their covenant. Once clients become aware of the time limitations, they have a much better idea of how to pace themselves during a counseling session.

The manner in which a pastoral counselor closes each interview deserves consideration. It is very risky to let a person get intensely anxious and then close the interview because the clock has gotten to a certain point. That causes clients to feel intimidated by the whole subject of counseling, and this may almost intolerably delay their efforts to work intently. One of the pastoral counselor's heaviest responsibilities is to try to help the client reduce anxiety before the end of a session.[1]

In general terms, adherence to the original time limit will curtail a manipulative client's dominating tendencies, reassure opposite-sex (or homosexual) clients of the minister's wholesome intentions, and encourage shy, passive clients that the time is really theirs to use as best they can. On those rare occasions when an extension of the time limit seems appropriate, this change should be mentioned directly, discussed, and jointly agreed upon, not just done. Thus the relationship is open, honest, trustworthy, and dependable. While the time issue may be microscopic compared to the problems at hand, it gives the client the opportunity to express the feelings and patterns of behavior with which he or she responds to the larger issues.

One rule for closing an interview is to start tapering off in intensity a few minutes before the scheduled end. Certain techniques suggested for actually bringing the interview to a close, are (1) referring to the time limits; (2) summarizing the important features of the session; (3) scheduling a future appointment; (4) suggesting some homework: something to read, do, or think about; (5) making subtle gestures of preparation to leave such as looking at the door or clock; (6) standing up; and (7) moving to the door and opening it. The main goal when terminating an interview is to consolidate what has been achieved into some durable benefit for the client.[2]

Clients who share intimate feelings, and especially those who confess something of a sinful nature, should be reassured of the counselor's continued respect. Pastoral counselors might want to thank clients for the confidence placed in them by discussing such painful areas and remind them that these matters will be held in confidence. This action strengthens a relationship that might otherwise disintegrate between interviews.

Occasionally clients make some very significant and potent statements just as they leave the counseling room. Perhaps the pressure of leaving motivates them to say what they had been thinking all during the interview. At times it seems as though, in doing this, a client has tossed an emotional bomb with a lighted fuse into the room on the way out. For example, just before she closed the door and left, one of my clients said, "You know, I thought I had been doing pretty well at evading my problem of frigidity in our sessions, but actually I know that I have talked about it one way or another every time." By taking note of departing statements such as this one, counselors usually can introduce them appropriately during the succeeding interview.

TERMINATING THE COUNSELING RELATIONSHIP

The client's final learning experience from the therapeutic relationship is a constructive, creative leave-taking of both the counselor and the counseling situation. Termination forces clients to find that they can bear both the fear and the pain of withdrawal from a depth of union perhaps never risked since birth and weaning, and it forces them to discover within themselves the rightful substitute. Their interaction between the will to unite and the will to separate is continuous from the first interview to the last. Yet there occurs in clients the general trend that moves them to the final point of rejecting the supporting relationship and asserting the independent self.

Pastoral counselors have a unique problem regarding termination. In going about pastoral duties, they normally have far more post-counseling contacts and conversations with clients than "secular" therapists. Former clients continue to feel friendly toward their pastor, but they no longer have the desperate need for the therapeutic relationship they may have felt earlier. This will be discussed further in the next chapter.

Pastors must understand that people regret leaving situations that have been satisfying or rewarding. For this reason pastoral counselors try to take great care to see that the intensity of the positive transference is sufficiently diminished in the later stages of therapy in order to permit a leave-taking that is not too traumatic.

Otto Rank probably emphasized the importance of the method of termination more than any other early writer in the field. He saw in the termination of therapy a trauma of separation similar to the birth trauma. He wrote that in the end phase of the therapeutic process, the therapist, who has been seen by the client as an assistant ego, has now come to be seen as a real ego. He advised: "This giving up of the assistant-ego, with simultaneous acceptance of reality, appears to me as the most important problem of therapy, for the solution of which careful preparation must be made in advance."[3]

Clients often ask their pastoral counselors in early interviews how long the counseling process might take. Many ministers are unwilling at such an early point to risk committing themselves to a guess at the termination date. However, according to a number of experimental studies reviewed by Jerome Frank, the speed of improvement may often be largely determined by client expectancy as conveyed to them by their counselors. The studies also showed that a favorable response to brief therapy may be enduring.[4]

By the time the counseling situation is ready to be terminated, the relationship has come to have great meaning for clients. Thus ending may arouse some anxiety. I agree with Ronald Lee, who stated that as a general rule, the longer the pastoral therapy lasts, the greater the number of sessions necessary to terminate.[5] Clients in these situations need their counselors to help them express this anxiety rather than to interpret these responses as a need for further treatment. Pastoral counselors must be willing to terminate counseling and to allow the relationship to their clients to recede into a more nominal pastor-parishioner relationship.

Generally the counseling process will terminate spontaneously. A series of elaborate studies of counseling indicated that client responses tended to become more positive and self-directive toward the end of counseling. The counselor can look for other client clues to effect closure: (1) indications that the general goals of counseling, such as insight and understanding, have been accomplished; (2) intellectual awareness of a solution and direction to the problem; (3) diminution of such factors as anxiety; and (4) behavior improvement. The counselors in the study terminated counseling when they felt that the goals had been achieved, or when lack of progress, in their opinion, did not warrant continuation of the counseling. Once the problem was delimited, many counselors structured the time limits in such a way that when this limit was reached, closure proceedings began.[6]

Clients terminate counseling themselves for many reasons. These include disruptions caused by client resistance; time limitations; scheduling problems; ignorance about counseling; anxiety or trauma; cost; and the feeling that the counselor is no longer needed. Pastoral counselors often set higher goals for their clients than the clients set for themselves. Clients sometimes make several abortive attempts to operate alone with a few newly discovered insights, only to be forced to return later.

Verbal preparation is the first step in terminating a series of interviews. When pastoral counselors feel the point of maximum benefit approaching, they can begin to listen for expressions of a similar opinion from their clients and agree with them. Instead of maintaining an asymmetrical relationship in which the client is primarily the talker and the minister the listener, the minister may establish a more egalitarian relationship in which he or she may talk more but interpret less.[7]

Karl Menninger warned that "some patients, once the date of termination is more or less tentatively agreed on mutually, will suddenly become very much 'sicker.' Many symptoms will recur, as if the unconscious were protesting vigorously the arbitrary decision of the ego. Usually what is necessary is merely the postponement of the date."[8]

One natural technique that I like to use for terminating a series of interviews is to taper off gradually. A client who has been having an appointment once each week is reduced to one every other week, then once every three weeks, and so on until formal leave-taking seems appropriate. Meeting less frequently helps to consolidate the gains while reducing intensity or dependency in the relationship.

Since ministers serving as pastors of a congregation continue to see the church members they have counseled, they cannot completely terminate their relationships with these people. Nevertheless, pastors can aid client adjustment back into church life by accepting a nonextravagant gift, if offered; directing the client's feelings of affection or hostility Godward; and providing specific occasions and ways for the growing person to serve God in the church. Thus pastors can transfer their clients' deepest feelings toward God and his gracious purpose for individual lives.[9]

When formal termination of the counseling situation actually occurs, the counselor should enable the client to feel as free to return as to stay in counseling. Clients need to be aware that if an obvious need arises, they should not spend too much energy trying to avoid returning. They should know that the minister is available if real difficulties arise. The benefits of the therapeutic experience emerge in part from the client's awareness that this intensive relationship is begun with the idea that it will end eventually and a normal pastor-parishioner relationship will resume. Thus the termination phase of counseling becomes a process of affirming or reaffirming the difference clients may perceive in themselves as they have developed in the minister-client relationship.

The ending of a counseling relationship brings to the pastoral counselor the satisfaction of having helped another person, but it also often brings the humbling recognition that not all that had been hoped for has been accomplished. Moreover, honest counselors usually recognize that in helping others, they also have been helped. The pastoral counselor can be grateful to the Spirit of God, whose power made possible whatever change was accomplished.[10]

PART III:
WHAT ARE THE IMPLICATIONS
OF RELATIONSHIP FOR PASTORS?

Most of a pastor's communication involves pastoral care that does not really constitute counseling. For example, many of a minister's conversations might accurately be called "precounseling" interaction. In his book on pastoral care, Paul E. Johnson regards relationship as the key to the vocation of the pastor as well as the heart of pastoral counseling.[1] On this basis one can readily see that a pastor can use counseling skills in various situations outside the formal counseling context.

The purpose of this last section of the book is to suggest some implications of the pastoral counseling relationship and apply them to the more general work of pastoral care. My assumption here is that dealing with a few individuals in depth ought to provide certain general principles for ministering meaningfully to larger numbers of people.

Chapter 13

Counseling Acquaintances:
A Unique Problem for the Minister

Pastoral experience apart from counseling abounds with instances of persons thinking about and feeling toward their pastors as they previously felt toward parental figures. Thus transference, both negative and positive, occurs in many church situations. Pastors often evoke this response without seeking it or understanding it, but merely by living out a role that repeats patterns that people encountered in childhood. Leslie Moser states that "people constantly transfer other personalities onto their friends and acquaintances."[1] Previously Freud had explained it another way: "Transference arises spontaneously in all human relationships. . . . It is everywhere the true vehicle of therapeutic influence; and the less its presence is suspected, the more powerfully it operates."[2]

The phenomenon of transference leads many in the psychotherapeutic field to maintain that therapists should not accept relatives, friends, or acquaintances as clients. But pastors are often asked to counsel those they know well. This can be accomplished by following some general guidelines.

PRECOUNSELING CONTACTS

Seward Hiltner observed that "most of the pastor's professional contacts are not counseling in the narrower sense but are precounseling pastoral work."[3] The phenomenon of client "pre-selection" is one of the major factors that draw people to ministers for counseling. Many people come to their ministers because they represent the church and religion. Thus there seems to be a strong likelihood of a preformed transference, or perhaps even countertransference phenomenon, in the pastoral counseling relationship because of the religious and cultural role of the minister.

According to Brister, the precounseling activities of the minister include (1) social contacts in the community, church, hospital, and elsewhere; (2) supportive calls, often accompanied by prayer, in the hospital or home; (3) teaching, frequently initiated by the pastor to prepare persons for church membership or for marriage; (4) interviews, for the purpose of interpreting some ecclesiastical or doctrinal matter, or some passage of Scripture; (5) disciplinary conversations; (6) confessional interviews, in which the person has revealed feelings of shame, guilt, hostility, anxiety, and so on in a single conversation; (7) consultative conversations with staff members, fellow ministers, or other professional persons in behalf of some individual or family; (8) administrative conversations with church leaders and workers concerning various programs and functions of the church; and (9) preaching and leading services of worship.[4]

Precounseling conversations may be distinguished from actual counseling by their comparatively short duration, the initiative and responsibility the minister may take in such interviews, the range of settings in which they occur, and the immediacy of the concerns compared with the problems discussed in counseling that have developed over any number of years. These precounseling conversations should not be minimized, because from the client's perspective they are usually very significant. Individual needs for ordering personal existence, for spiritual strength, and for clarification of direction may be as urgent in a single, informal interview as in multiple-interview counseling.

In precounseling contacts with people, pastors do well not to become so friendly and close to individuals that they can no longer minister effectively as pastor or counselor if a serious problem develops. Some pastors try to base their ministry on friendships. Perhaps this course of action is even expected by people in rural and small-town churches. Such pastors enter their members' homes from the back door without knocking, pour their own coffee, sit down at the kitchen table, kick off their shoes, and still try to be objective enough to minister to that family. A pastor may adopt this "preacher boy" mentality to give the illusion of being an ideal son for the family or to attempt to meet the family's need to have someone be dependent on them. Such a minister, however, would probably have great difficulty moving out of the level of a friendly relationship into a counseling relationship, if in fact he or she is able to do so at all.

The pastor should usually refuse to "bootleg"—that is, give counseling under the guise of some other type of relationship. Consider this example from my own experience. When I was doing supervisory clinical pastoral education in a mental hospital, I was befriended by a social work student who came to see me quite often under the guise of discussing religious problems. I eventually wondered if this might not be a substitute for therapy. When I consulted the social worker who was supervising some of my pastoral counseling, she felt strongly that the young man (whom she had been trying to get into therapy) should be confronted with the reality of the situation. With some reluctance, I confronted the student. He became quite angry after a few minutes and vowed to end the friendship. Nevertheless, he later began psychotherapy, and we resumed the pastoral friendship with different dimensions.

Precounseling is also the term applied to the first interview that pastors have with potential clients. Too much so-called nondirectiveness on the part of pastors at this time actually could doom the relationship, because clients might find it meaningless. Counselors are always faced with the responsibility of knowing how to make the best use of one hour, and unlike other therapists, pastors have to do their own "intake interviews." It is during this first interview—the precounseling interview—that pastors must appraise the situation.

Even before the first interview, however, a clue as to some of the components of client attitudes may be discernible. If Miss Jones comes to see her pastor voluntarily on the recommendation of a friend who was formerly a client, it is very likely that she is prepared to be treated as her friend was. If her friend took psychological tests, she expects to take them. If her friend liked Reverend Smith, she probably expects to like him too, and no long process of "breaking the ice" is necessary. A completely different example would be Bill, a troubled youth whose parents required that he seek counseling from the pastor because of repeated disobedience at school. In this case we can expect Bill to regard the pastor as one of the authorities who does not understand him and who is against him.

An interesting experimental study of precounseling was conducted with twenty-six persons on a waiting list for therapy in a counseling center. These people provided repeated Q-sort descriptions of themselves, and the study found the same general improvement trends among those on the waiting list who had had no counseling as for those who had had successful counseling. The subjects' self-concept tended to become more positive and more consistent, and the self-ideal became more positive than it had been previously. Of course, in all cases these alterations were of a smaller magnitude than those reported in counseling.[5] On the basis of this study, the pastor's precounseling work can be inferred to be highly significant and helpful.

COUNSELING ACQUAINTANCES

The minister has both formal contacts, as pastor with parishioners in the church, and informal contacts, as friend and neighbor with people in the community. Mixing these two types of contacts indiscriminately often leads to confused relationships. Thus ministers need to think through the unique problem of counseling acquaintances.

Psychoanalysts have characteristically refused to accept as patients anyone with whom they have had prior social contacts. Freud wrote:

> Special difficulties arise when the analyst and his new patient or their families are on terms of friendship or have social ties with one another. The psycho-analyst [sic] who is asked to undertake the treatment of wife or child of a friend must be prepared for it to cost him that friendship, no matter what the outcome of the treatment may be; nevertheless he must make the sacrifice if he cannot find a trustworthy substitute.[6]

Freud felt that an analyst's objectivity with patients is very important. For example, as his friends knew, Freud had an intense interest in Egyptology. Once he suspected he was becoming too fascinated with the subject to objectively help a patient who was an Egyptologist. His professional integrity demanded that he send the man to another analyst less interested in Egyptology.[7] Similarly, Rabbi Henry E. Kagan, who holds a doctorate in clinical psychology, stated that he has never counseled with a member of his congregation of five hundred families at Sinai Temple in Mount Vernon, New York. He offers his counseling ministry only to persons referred to him by other rabbis.[8]

Can the pastor counsel effectively with church members, friends, and acquaintances? Hiltner made a distinction between friendship and friendliness. Friendliness plainly refers to warmth, genuine interest, and real concern for people, which is as important in counseling as in any other pastoral relationship. Friendship is not merely a relationship to which the pastor gives something, but also one from which he receives. Thus counseling is not friendship. The essence of counseling is that two people agree to concentrate their attention on the problems, interests, concerns, and values of one.[9] Counseling can be satisfactorily conducted if the therapeutic contacts are kept strictly separate from the occasional friendly contacts.

There are at least three differences between being a counselor and being a friend. First, a counselor's training allows him or her to understand another person's psychological difficulties much better than a friend usually understands. Second, the therapeutic relationship is not mutual. The interests, problems, and welfare of clients always come first, while counselors in return merely ask for consideration of personal needs. Counselors do not ordinarily respond to anger or criticism defensively or decide whether to continue the relationship on the basis of the pleasantness of the client's company. Third, formalities such as office appointments and fees seldom characterize friendships.[10]

The therapy relationship is different from most close relationships in that it is more structured. It includes certain times (fifty-minute sessions) and a certain place (counselor's office), is task-oriented (to improve the counselee's well-being), and it is meant to end or change when it has been successful.[11]

There is no general reason why pastors cannot temporarily redefine the relationship with personal friends and become, for a time, their counselor. Carl Rogers stated his belief that clients "can meet the counselor socially or professionally during or after therapy with little effect beyond what is normally involved in the immediate reality of their relationship."[12] In such a situation, the greatest confusion stems from pastors' inability to recognize their own emotional need to continue to receive something from the relationship. The covenant-making aspects of counseling with friends might take the following dimensions:

> You and I have been close friends and there are a lot of things we can take for granted together. But we're not talking merely as friends now. We are talking about you and trying to help you get over this rough experience you've had so that, whatever you do in the future, you'll know better what's going on.

Treating one's personal acquaintances certainly is not entirely disadvantageous. In fact, there are several obvious advantages. The counselor knows these friends on the basis of witnessed, overt behavior. Furthermore, motivation to help is strong because of the friendship. Finally, rapport and relationship are ready-made at the beginning of counseling.

Of course, ministers are not able to formally counsel members of their families or even very close friends. Pastors are at least partially responsible for the conduct of their families, and close friendships characteristically are reciprocal situations of both giving to and getting from one another. The "more the counselor is responsible for a person's standard of conduct outside of therapy, the more difficult it may be for the client to be free and self-responsible during the therapy hours."[13]

There are three factors which contribute to the potential for a harmful dual relationship for clergy who serve both as congregational ministers and as pastoral counselors for church members. First, personality characteristics common to many clergy can make setting boundaries difficult. Such pastors are people-pleasers who need to be needed. Second, one of the major rewards appreciated by many ministers is the praise and adoration of others. The most popular clergy may be those who abide by the least amount of boundaries or limits and are always available and willing to set aside family and personal considerations in order to "help" church people. Third, a professional image of selflessness and service along with limited self-awareness can make pastors who counsel vulnerable to using their clients to meet some of their own needs.[14]

Nevertheless, if the therapeutic relationship is not altogether different from other kinds of relationships, such as friendships, then pastors are able to help clients who are also church members. Pastors will naturally be associated—individually and socially, privately and publicly—with many of those who come for counseling. In addition, sometimes during the process of counseling, pastors receive invitations to dinner or requests to make home visits or to minister to other family members. A pastor's spouse usually has social affiliations with clients as well.

The pastor is not the only type of counselor who has contacts with clients apart from the counseling situation. It holds, for instance, of counselors who are also teachers in an academic setting. William Snyder described as follows some of his counseling as a professor of psychology at Pennsylvania State University:

> One client did his assistantship work under the therapist's supervision for part of the time he was in therapy, and one client was supervised in his own therapeutic work by the therapist while the client was in therapy with him. We certainly do not feel that these contaminations of the therapy relationship were ideal; under the circumstances they seem inescapable. They made the therapeutic task a little more difficult for both therapist and clients. The fact is, however, that despite these dual roles of the therapist, the therapeutic relationship usually managed to remain not seriously contaminated.[15]

How does a pastor go about counseling acquaintances? The counseling relationship is essentially the pastoral relationship, deepened and intensified for a relatively short period of time in order to deal with some specific problems. The difference is quantitative, not qualitative. Following an exploratory interview, the participants agree on a more formal counseling relationship with the recognition that at the conclusion of the special and temporary relationship, they will resume the general pastoral relationship. The covenant concerning the counseling relationship is such that the client takes the major responsibility for continuing the sessions or for reopening them at a later time. Theoretically the pastor-parishioner relationship that includes counseling, when viewed in linear fashion, entails (1) sharing personally prior to counseling; (2) entering the client's private world in a more formal counseling relationship; (3) appraising the client's situation; (4) examining the person's plight in Christian perspective; and (5) terminating counseling and resuming a less formal pastoral relationship.

Hiltner suggested that the shift from the general pastoral relationship to the pastoral counseling relationship is difficult in proportion to the pastor's hesitation to acknowledge the shift explicitly. The pastor who hesitates to do so permits the nature of the counseling relationship to remain partially ambiguous. "Once in the open and articulated, it is our experience that there is little difference from any other counseling."[16]

Two other aspects of this subject have already been mentioned but bear repeating. First, not only are pastors previously acquainted with many clients, but they also have social contacts with those clients' spouses, relatives, and friends. Karl Menninger wrote that "out of laziness, or lack of self-confidence, many analysts refuse to see close relatives, thereby handicapping their efforts with the patients."[17] What Menninger meant is that concerned therapists like to get acquainted with the family of their patients. Pastors need not feel overcautious about doing so either.

The other aspect is that pastors need to recognize that while they must be very discreet about counseling conversations, their clients may feel free to discuss vividly their verbal interchanges. Pastoral counselors must keep this in mind so that their words, when repeated, will contribute to, rather than detract from, their general ministry.

POSTCOUNSELING CONTACTS

The pastor obviously does not stop general contact with parishioner clients at the termination of the counseling process. Rather, the relationship with the client shifts back to the more normal dimensions of pastor and church member. The relationship-focused pastoral counselor does more than hope that this will automatically happen. The following is an explicit discussion of the process of the shift with the client.

While some clients will join the church that is served by their pastoral counselor, in a few instances pastors have lost members whom they were trying to help through counseling. This may be because occasionally clients who "confess all" are unable to face their confessors later. Partly for this reason the Roman Catholic Church allows for priests to be concealed from view in the confessional booth. To this end, Hiltner and Colston suggest the following:

> The shame-on-later-meeting response is true only to the degree that the special relationship has been cathartic—getting it off the chest—in nature and not also assimilative—accepting, clarifying, and hence making a new decision about. In Hiltner's experience, the extent to which ex-parishioners with whom he counseled subsequently avoid him is due in part to his own deficiencies as counselor but more to whether he succeeded in working the problem through or not. If he worked it through, they know his memory of it is much more of resolution than of disclosure. The shame of psychic nudity has been dissolved into sympathetic understanding of pilgrimage.[18]

In my opinion, two additional factors are important. As I have stated, ministers should not allow clients to confess too much too soon. Sometimes such clients, having opened the floodgates, have difficulty closing them and thus allow too much dirty water to spill out. Occasionally the anxiety aroused in clients by confronting too nondirective and silent a counselor forces them to say more than they really intended. In this process the client's motivation for further counseling is drained, yet there has not been enough time for the relationship to develop acceptance and understanding. Thus these clients have a difficult time either facing the pastor ("I don't know what he may think of me") or returning for another interview ("I don't know what all he may pull out of me next time").

My other concern deals with the pastoral motivation for hearing such confessional material. If clients suspect that their pastors could ever possibly expose them, or if those pastors actually think less of their clients as persons after having heard their morbid confessions, it is natural that the clients consider the wisdom of joining a different church.

Concerning the posttherapeutic relationship, psychiatrist Jules Masserman writes:

If the therapy is well conducted and neurotic transferences appropriately dissolved, the patient and therapist may continue on a basis of the same sort of mutual respect and friendship permissible and desirable in any other field of medicine. This relationship, however, should include neither unresolved hatreds nor excessive glorifications or loyalties on the part of the patient, and neither professional avoidance nor exploitation on the part of the therapist. Indeed, any therapist with a coterie of adoring ex-patients perennially clustered about him may be suspect on that basis alone. However, a certain amount of gratitude for help rendered is a natural and healthy reaction, and need embarrass neither patient nor therapist.[19]

Several things are at stake in the follow-up stage of pastoral counseling. First, overdependence is often a problem that needlessly brings clients back to the pastors again and again. Pastors can do nothing more effective than to tutor such clients in the art of prayer and the practice of leaning on God for strength. Also, fear and hostility may be a problem if a pastor maintains a perfectionistic goal for the clients to achieve without fail. Finally, gossip will be a hazard for pastors who have a tendency to tell others any of what was said during counseling sessions.

The first few postcounseling contacts after formal termination are crucial. The pastor should be alert for signs of avoidance, such as atypical disappearance during or immediately after worship services, or the avoidance of eye contact. Some clients retain a feeling of embarrassment upon seeing the pastor. The problem can usually be resolved if the pastor will initiate a few comfortable social contacts or maybe discuss this concern in a telephone call during the first weeks after counseling ends.[20]

Some pastors will not receive a fee for counseling. The professional counselor has a fee structure through which clients regularly express gratitude by payment. Some pastors, rather than taking this course of action, attempt to help clients focus their gratitude on God-in-Christ and on the church. However, pastors should not ignore the significance of a client's desire to express gratitude tangibly. Joining the church, volunteering for Christian service, complimenting the pastor, or giving a gift all have a part in fulfilling an

obligation the client feels. These things also help resolve any transference that may have arisen in the process of counseling.

The "Code of Ethics" of the American Association of Pastoral
Counselors speaks to many of the issues discussed in this chapter. It
is included in Appendix B and should be carefully studied.

Chapter 14

Pastoral Work

Pastoral work is founded on the structure of relationship in New Testament teachings and practices. For pastors, the influences of relationship are inseparable from the quest for the will of God in people's affairs. Counselor-client relationships are a supplement to this major quest in pastoral work.

Thomas W. Klink of the Menninger Foundation suggested an "encounter" as the basic unit of pastoral work. He used this term to refer to the distinctive moments of meeting and acknowledging the meaningful existence of another (in person or even through long-distance communication) that mark the life of ministry. In an encounter, more or less explicit expectations emerge within a continuing and often multifaceted relationship. After any specific pastoral service contract is fulfilled, the continuing relationship is resumed, even though perhaps modified. This concept of encounter is used to place pastoral work on the broadest possible base.[1]

GENERAL PASTORAL RELATIONSHIPS

Carroll Wise notes that the "general pastoral relationship is the keystone in the entire arch of the minister's many activities."[2] Ministers achieve success probably as much by *being* a certain kind of person as by *doing* certain things. Yet ministers seldom think of their relationship with others as a resource; instead they often wish they could "think of something to say or do that would help." Ministers who exude attitudes of empathic understanding, reverence, genuineness, and concreteness in both formal and informal relationships usually are considered by parishioners to be helpful in every phase of ministry. Rollo May wrote that "in every human contact some molding of personality occurs."[3]

The therapeutic relationship is but one example of interpersonal relations. Carl Rogers maintains that the same laws govern all relationships. Thus if a parent, teacher, administrator, or clergy is able to create the right kind of psychological atmosphere for the child, student, staff member, or church member, then a more wholesome relationship exists.[4] In F. E. Fiedler's experimental study of relationship, the fact that even laypeople could describe the ideal therapeutic relationship in terms which correlated highly with those of the experts suggests that "a good therapeutic relationship is very much like any [other] good relationship."[5]

Therefore, a ministry through relationships is possible when pastors offer not a set of dogmas or an institutional program, but themselves in relationship. These relationships are quite significant, since ministers traditionally represent God-in-Christ. Such ministers come to measure effectiveness by the quality of interpersonal relationships.

However, pastoral ministry through relationships to individuals, to small groups, and to large groups often is hampered by transference. Historically, the ministry, according to psychiatrist Edgar Draper, is the only profession that has encouraged transference by having its constituents address its members as "father" or "brother." Ministers offer the world, and especially parishioners, a figure loaded with the potential for illogical response. A minister's arrival on the scene usually brings group behavior changes, household rearrangements, new conversational directions, and looks of surprise. Although pastors learn to live with these reactions and sometimes to smile at them, all too often they are misunderstood.[6]

One incident that occurred when I was beginning a new pastorate illustrates this. I was visiting the rather young and attractive wife of an alcoholic with the hope of encouraging her to resume an active religious life. In trying to help me understand why she attended church so seldomly, she finally revealed that a former pastor of the church had tried to help her with her problems and as a result she felt she had fallen in love with him. She could no longer attend church without feeling very guilty, and she had avoided talking to subsequent ministers of the church.

This woman benefited greatly from an experience of God's forgiveness along with a token understanding of positive transference. However, if the former pastor involved with her had understood what was happening, the whole situation might have been avoided.

Paul Johnson called the work of pastors an "interpersonal vocation," suggesting that the pastoral role in society is defined by what others expect of pastors as they see them in relation to themselves. Pastors accomplish their work as they enter into significant value-making relationships with persons human and divine. In keeping with the ministerial call, pastors are expected to mediate as the reconciling agent between human persons and the divine in the interest of better relationships for all.[7]

DYNAMIC PASTORAL COMMUNICATION

Dynamic pastoral communication is necessary for genuine interpersonal dialogue and understanding. "Dynamic" implies the dimensions of depth in human development and the energetic forces at work in interpersonal relationships. "Pastoral" describes the contextual nature of the minister-person connection. "Communication" suggests the give and take of interpersonal dialogue, yet includes many nonverbal factors. Of course, not all human contacts constitute counseling when viewed in terms of time and intensity, but all may in principle partake of its nature.

Dynamic pastoral communication normally operates during all the pastor's experiences with people day in and day out. A careful vocational analysis reveals that a pastor speaks primarily in the language of the interpersonal encounter. The lines of ministry are drawn primarily, but not exclusively, along person-to-person contacts and person-with-group encounters. Thus the central function of the pastor is essentially that of communication. Communication dominates in preaching, teaching, pastoral care and counseling, and in the various administrative functions of the pastoral office.

It is appropriate to note the differences between the pastor's social, advisement, counseling, and therapeutic conversations. Each of these has a conversational setting as a common element. But each has a different purpose. In their book *The Counseling Relationship,* Arnold Buchheimer and Sarah Carter Balogh show that the differences are easily detected. The purpose of the *social conversation* is to maintain distortions. The person plays a role that he or she consciously or unconsciously desires to maintain, whether or not it actually represents the person. For instance, Jim will say to his friend, "I want to get into an Ivy League school, but I probably won't." His friend replies, "Oh, you always worry! You'll get in."

Advisement conversation is related to a set of predetermined conditions. People are confronted with their capacity to meet certain conditions and with the possibility and probability of meeting them. These conditions may be, for example, grades in relation to a college admissions policy, or a set of skills and aptitudes in relation to the job market. Some facet of individuals—some sample of their behavior—is abstracted out of them, is considered representative of them, and is then related to a set of general conditions.

The *counseling conversation* is the setting in which clients express their point of view toward the world. The assumption in counseling is that this point of view is distorted and that through the counseling conversation process, people will revise their distortions and thereafter alter their behavior. The emphasis is on the present and on verbal material that is within the person's immediate awareness or comprehensibility. For instance, a high school senior will say, "My biggest hope is to get into an Ivy League school." The counselor may perceive the boy's doubts and reflect these as part of the counseling process. The boy's doubts may be real, or they may be a function of an inadequate view of himself as he is at present.

In *therapeutic conversation,* the approach is historic and symbolic, relying heavily on the reactivation and consideration of unconscious information. Here the basic content of conversation is the consideration of past experiences and the reconstruction of what happened and what has been repressed to cause distortions of the present. In the case of the boy who would like to attend an Ivy League college, the therapist would deal with the boy's doubts by examining parental relationships and past experiences that have caused him to be uncertain of himself. The therapist would assume that the client's doubts were a distortion of the present and a symptom of deeper problems of pervasive self-mistrust.[8]

The specific nature of pastoral communication may be summarized as follows: Pastoral conversation takes place because the church—and through the church, Christ—has commissioned the pastor. Pastoral communication reaches its goal when people know themselves to be in God's presence. Pastoral conversation may cover a wide range of topics, not just theological matters.[9] Entering such encounters requires that the pastor master the skills of initiating genuine conversation, understanding by active listening, inviting the other person to speak by hearing him or her out, and demonstrating Christian concern in an impersonal culture.[10]

Some pastors with certain personality patterns have difficulty building meaningful relationships of any kind. People are uncertain about turning to a perfectionist who leaves the impression that "real" Christians never have problems, or to a rigid authoritarian who never sees more than one side to any story. They also shy away from the "cocky debunker" who always tries to impress people rather than minister to them, as well as the preoccupied administrator who uses people in order to operate the church successfully.[11]

CHRISTIAN WORSHIP

The pastor who approaches sermon preparation each week with the question "What shall I preach?" is not apt to speak directly to the people. Instead the approach should be, "To whom will I be speaking, and what are their needs?" The pastor will not be able to set souls ablaze with purpose with a series of unrelated abstractions. The skilled pastor instructs people in the celebration of worship, at the same time recognizing individual differences within the congregation and remembering the participants' concerns in corporate worship.

Pastors should implicitly acknowledge that preaching occurs in a context of worship. They should constructively and imaginatively attempt to relate communion with God in worship to conversations with people in society.

Russell L. Dicks, who was a pioneer in hospital chaplaincy, noted that a "good relationship is important in pastoral work and preaching because we do not think with our minds, but with our feelings; we are not moved by ideas, but by our emotions; we do not reach decisions with our heads, but with our hearts."[12]

Wayne Oates suggests that the pastor who maintains a counseling ministry will move in the direction of life-situation preaching. The characteristics of such preaching are fourfold: (1) the interpretation of human experience in the light of biblical truth rather than the exhortation of people to the observance of certain moral precepts as such; (2) the development of personal insight into the motives of personal and group action rather than condemnation of this or that kind of behavior; (3) the encouragement of parishioners toward faith in God, in one another, and in themselves as a means of gaining control over behavior that they themselves discover to be alien to the mind of Christ; and (4) the growth of a sense of comradeship with God-in-Christ and a change in personality through this transforming friendship.[13]

This kind of preaching produces a cyclical movement. The preaching becomes a preparation for counseling, and the therapeutic relationships developed in pastoral care and counseling lend feeling and meaning to preaching.

Just *how much* counseling sessions can lead to sermon preparation is worth examining. Counseling pastors do well to follow certain ground rules in planning to use occasional illustrations from counseling in sermons. First, it is appropriate to use illustrations that point to positive, inspiring, and heroic traits in clients but not to derogatory or cynically humorous attitudes pastors may have toward clients. Second, pastors should always get permission from the persons involved before using this information, and they should acknowledge the permission. Third, even counseling pastors will get most illustrations from literary sources, with only occasional illustrations coming from counseling sessions. Fourth, pastors should not try to turn preaching into a counseling session. Finally, the pastoral attitudes expressed through preaching indirectly should encourage people to have confidence in them as counselors.

The good shepherd of the flock tries to communicate his or her essence, for people often view the church the same way they view their pastors. Of course, the preacher actually communicates in two ways: one by what the mouth says, the other by what the body does. If the pastor identifies with the flock in such a way as to admit to being sinful also, this helps the people to identify with the pastor as well. Apparently people are better able to listen to a person who is struggling with problems similar to their own than they are able to accept "hand-me-down" advice of a "higher-up." The content and delivery of the preacher's message is closely connected to his or her personal conscious or unconscious needs. The preacher may use the pulpit to flay and flog the people, to get them to support a new idea, or to bring about spiritual insight and peace. Consequently the emotional needs of particular preachers are a major factor in cementing or inhibiting the interpersonal relationship with the people listening.[14]

If pastors listen intently to people through the week during times of pastoral care and counseling and thus are able to form meaningful relationships with them, the parishioners will in turn be better able to listen intently to sermons and relate meaningfully to the pastor. Thus congregations may perceive their ministers not only as talking preachers, but also as listening pastors.

PASTORAL CARE AND VISITATION

The pastoral ministry is primarily a relationship between those who are called to a special role within the household of faith and those people of God who at times have special needs requiring skillful attention. For those outside the fellowship, God's purpose is that they be "found" and in the process find themselves. "Pastoral care" refers to relationships between the various ministries of the church and its individuals or families. In pastoral care relationships, the goal is to help the people involved live more effectively with themselves in the presence of God and in the company of God's people.[15]

The aims of pastoral care remain very similar to those of the church: bringing people to Christ and the Christian fellowship, aiding them to repent of sin and to accept God's salvation, helping them to live with themselves and their community in brotherhood and love, and enabling them to act in faith and confidence.

Visitation is as much a part of the shepherding tradition of the ministry as any other activity. It is a vital aspect of ministry in which the pastor's concern is communicated in a personal way. Some pastoral visits prompt deeper-level counseling, while some simply remain friendly encounters, such as welcoming newcomers to the neighborhood after having been separated from their familiar surroundings and as they face adjustments in a new community. Brister lists three major types of pastoral visits: (1) *routine calls,* in which the church's message and fellowship are carried regularly to persons and families; (2) *crucial calls,* in which Christian resources are offered to those in crises or distress, and (3) *casual contacts,* in which the pastor encounters people in unstructured settings, yet seeks to make such contacts vital. Pastors may make contacts through telephone calls, correspondence, or visits in homes, hospitals, businesses, or other public places.[16]

Even though many pastors have practically given up pastoral visitation and others have concentrated on making many superficial contacts, the relationship-focused pastor's main concern remains the depth of the interpersonal relationship during the visit. Unfortunately many clergy merely use pastoral visitation as a means to get people to come to church on Sunday, overlooking the fact that the visit can be meaningful and helpful in itself. As Carroll Wise observed, the "basic purpose of calling is to develop and maintain a close pastoral relationship with the people in the parish."[17]

Pastoral counselors who build ministry on relationships rather than friendships are able to extend pastoral care to both strangers and acquaintances, not by being "buddies," but by being professionals. By being professional, pastors are neither too close nor too distant to help. This kind of relationship, based on genuine concern for people, radiates the very presence of Christ.

Appendix A

AAPC Membership Information and Requirements

The two types of membership within the American Association of Pastoral Counselors (AAPC) are certified and non-certified, with sub-categories in each. All membership levels have specific requirements which must be met before submitting an application for membership.

CERTIFIED CATEGORIES

Certified categories of membership include Diplomate, Fellow, and Member Associate, the latter a provisionally certified level.

Educational preparation for certified membership should contribute to the pastoral counselor's training and develop a broad experience-related understanding of people. This should take place in a setting in which the pastor can relate theoretical knowledge to, and derive from, pastoral work with people, i.e., a setting in which both the school and practical situation are in mutual relation.

MEMBER ASSOCIATE (provisional certification):

Persons applying for Member Associate are usually those who have recently completed a training program in Pastoral Counseling. Often a person may have the formal requirements for Fellow category but lack the seasoning qualities that come from extended practice and experience. The certification of this apprentice membership category is provisional as the Members Associate moves toward full certification as Fellow. This is to be accomplished within seven years.

Member Associate applications receive a paper review. Persons elected to Member Associate will be required to meet the Regional

Membership Committee for a personal consultative interview following approval.

Requirements for Member Associate are: BA and MDiv, Masters or Doctoral level degree in theological or biblical studies, or in Pastoral Counseling from accredited schools; endorsement as a minister in good standing in a recognized religious body; continuing responsible relationship to local religious community; completion of a supervised self-reflective pastoral experience, the most common of which is one unit of clinical pastoral education; three years as a minister; 375 hours of pastoral counseling together with 125 hours of supervision of that counseling with one-third of such supervision to have been with an AAPC approved Training Program in Pastoral Counseling or from a Diplomate of the Association; and submission of a plan for becoming fully certified as a Fellow and/or Diplomate level within seven years.

The examination process for Diplomate and Fellow is a face-to-face interwew with a Regional Certification Committee. The Committee requires submission of clinical materials in preparation for the interview. Applications for Member Associate are approved in the Association office, followed by a consultative interview with the Regional Certification Committee.

FELLOW:

All the requirements for Member Associate plus: MA, STM, DMin or PhD in pastoral counseling or its equivalent; demonstrated ability to work as a pastoral counselor at an advanced level of competency; 1,000 hours of pastoral counseling while receiving at least 125 hours of supervision (totaling 1,375 hours of counseling and 250 hours of supervision).

Clinical Members and Supervisors certified by the American Association of Marriage and Family Therapists and doctoral level Clinical or Counseling Psychologists may make application for AAPC Fellow by showing evidence of AAMFT certification or evidence of state/provincial licensure (psychologists); endorsement as a minister in good standing in a recognized religious body; continuing responsible relationship to local religious community; and an integration of spiritual/pastoral dimension of clinical work.

DIPLOMATE:

All requirements for Fellow plus significant performance in at least three of the following—academic achievement (PhD or equivalent), research, publication, leadership in AAPC, teaching and/or supervising pastoral care/counseling, or contributions to church/community; also, supervision of at least five candidates for AAPC membership for a minimum of 30 hours each, while receiving 50 hours of personal supervision for the 150 cumulative hours supervised.

American Association of Pastoral Counselors
9508 A Lee Highway
Fairfax, Virginia 22031
703-385-6967

Appendix B

AAPC Code of Ethics*

(Amended April 28, 1994)
(Procedures separated out April 17, 1993✻)

PRINCIPLE I – PROLOGUE

As members‡ of the American Association of Pastoral Counselors, we are committed to the various theologies, traditions, and values of our faith communities and to the dignity and worth of each individual. We are dedicated to advancing the welfare of those who seek our assistance and to the maintenance of high standards of professional conduct and competence. We are accountable for our ministry whatever its setting. This accountability is expressed in relationships to clients, colleagues, students, our faith communities, and through the acceptance and practice of the principles and procedures of this Code of Ethics.

In order to uphold our standards, as members of AAPC we covenant to accept the following foundational premises:

---

*The AAPC Code of Ethics may be reproduced only after contacting the AAPC Association Office to ensure that the most current copy of the Code can be provided.

✻The AAPC Code of Ethics and the Ethics Committee Procedures were separated by action of the AAPC membership on April 17, 1993. The Board of Governors is now authorized to modify ethics committee procedures without further action by the membership. Members should note that the substantive rule from the Code of Ethics to be applied to an alleged violation will continue to be determined by the date of the alleged violation and not the date the complaint is received. However, as a result of the action taken, the current procedures in effect will be followed for all complaints brought after April 17, 1993, regardless of the date of alleged violation.

‡The use of "member," "we," "us," and "our" refers to and is binding upon all levels of individual and institutional membership and affiliation of AAPC.

A. To maintain responsible association with the faith group in which we have ecclesiastical standing.

B. To avoid discriminating against or refusing employment, educational opportunity, or professional assistance to anyone on the basis of race, gender, sexual orientation, religion, or national origin; provided that nothing herein shall limit a member or center from utilizing religious requirements or exercising a religious preference in employment decisions.

C. To remain abreast of new developments in the field through both educational activities and clinical experience. We agree at all levels of membership to continue post-graduate education and professional growth including supervision, consultation, and active participation in the meetings and affairs of the Association.

D. To seek out and engage in collegial relationships, recognizing that isolation can lead to a loss of perspective and judgment.

E. To manage our personal lives in a healthful fashion and to seek appropriate assistance for our own personal problems or conflicts.

F. To diagnose or provide treatment only for those problems or issues that are within the reasonable boundaries of our competence.

G. To establish and maintain appropriate professional relationship boundaries.

PRINCIPLE II – PROFESSIONAL PRACTICES

In all professional matters, members of AAPC maintain practices that protect the public and advance the profession.

A. We use our knowledge and professional associations for the benefit of the people we serve and not to secure unfair personal advantage.

B. We clearly represent our level of membership and limit our practice to that level.

C. Fees and financial arrangements, as well all contractual matters, are always discussed without hesitation or equivocation at the onset and are established in a straight-forward, professional manner.

D. We are prepared to render service to individuals and communities in crisis without regard to financial remuneration when necessary.

E. We neither receive nor pay a commission for referral of a client.

F. We conduct our practice, agency, regional, and Association fiscal affairs with due regard to recognized business and accounting procedures.

G. Upon the transfer of a pastoral counseling practice or the sale of real, personal, tangible, or intangible property or assets used in such practice, the privacy and well-being of the client shall be of primary concern.

   1. Client names and records shall be excluded from the transfer or sale.

   2. Any fees paid shall be for services rendered, consultation, equipment, real estate, and the name and logo of the counseling agency.

H. We are careful to represent facts truthfully to clients, referral sources, and third party payors regarding credentials and services rendered. We shall correct any misrepresentation of our professional qualifications or affiliations.

I. We do not malign colleagues or other professionals.

PRINCIPLE III – CLIENT RELATIONSHIPS

It is the responsibility of members of AAPC to maintain relationships with clients on a professional basis.

A. We do not abandon or neglect clients. If we are unable, or unwilling for appropriate reasons, to provide professional help or continue a professional relationship, every reasonable effort is made to arrange for continuation of treatment with another professional.

B. We make only realistic statements regarding the pastoral counseling process and its outcome.

C. We show sensitive regard for the moral, social, and religious standards of clients and communities. We avoid imposing our beliefs on others, although we may express them when appropriate in the pastoral counseling process.

D. Counseling relationships are continued only so long as it is reasonably clear that the clients are benefiting from the relationship.

E. We recognize the trust placed in and unique power of the therapeutic relationship. While acknowledging the complexity of some pastoral relationships, we avoid exploiting the trust and dependency of clients. We avoid these dual relationships with clients (e.g., business or close personal relationships) which could impair our professional judgment, compromise the integrity of the treatment, and/or use the relationship for our own gain.

F. We do not engage in harassment, abusive words or actions, or exploitative coercion of clients or former clients.

G. All forms of sexual behavior or harassment with clients are unethical, even when a client invites or consents to such behavior or involvement. Sexual behavior is defined as, but not limited to, all forms of overt and covert seductive speech, gestures, and behavior as well as physical contact of a sexual nature; harassment is defined as, but not limited to, repeated comments, gestures, or physical contacts of a sexual nature.

H. We recognize that the therapist/client relationship involves a power imbalance, the residual effects of which are operative following the termination of the therapy relationship. Therefore, all sexual behavior or harassment as defined in Principle III. G, with former clients is unethical.

PRINCIPLE IV – CONFIDENTIALITY

As members of AAPC, we respect the integrity and protect the welfare of all persons with whom we are working and have an obligation to safeguard information about them that has been obtained in the course of the counseling process.

A. All records kept on a client are stored or disposed of in a manner that assures security and confidentiality.

B. We treat all communications from clients with professional confidence.

C. Except in those situations where the identity of the client is necessary to the understanding of the case, we use only the first names of our clients when engaged in supervision or consultation. It is our responsibility to convey the importance of confidentiality to the supervisor/consultant; this is particularly important when the supervision is shared by other professionals, as in a supervisory group.

D. We do not disclose client confidences to anyone, except: as mandated by law; to prevent a clear and immediate danger to someone; in the course of a civil, criminal, or disciplinary action arising from the counseling where the pastoral counselor is a defendant; for purposes of supervision or consultation; or by previously obtained written permission. In cases involving more than one person (as client), written permission must be obtained from all legally accountable persons who have been present during the counseling before any disclosure can be made.

E. We obtain informed written consent of clients before audio and/or video tape recording or permitting third party observation of their sessions.

F. We do not use these standards of confidentiality to avoid intervention when it is necessary, e.g., when there is evidence of abuse of minors, the elderly, the disabled, the physically or mentally incompetent.

G. When current or former clients are referred to in a publication, while teaching, or in a public presentation, their identity is thoroughly disguised.

H. We as members of AAPC agree that as an express condition of our membership in the Association, Association ethics communications, files, investigative reports, and related records are strictly confidential and waive the right to use same in a court of law to advance any claim against another member. Any member seeking such records for such purpose shall be subject to disciplinary action for attempting to violate the confidentiality requirements of the organization. This policy is intended to promote pastoral and confessional communications without legal consequences and to protect potential privacy and confidentiality interest of third parties.

PRINCIPLE V – SUPERVISEE, STUDENT, AND EMPLOYEE RELATIONSHIPS

As members of AAPC, we have an ethical concern for the integrity and welfare of our supervisees, students, and employees. These relationships are maintained on a professional and confidential basis. We recognize our influential position with regard to both current and former supervisees, students, and employees, and avoid exploiting their trust and dependency. We make every effort to avoid dual relationships with such persons that could impair our judgment or increase the risk of personal and/or financial exploitation.

A. We do not engage in ongoing counseling relationships with current supervisees, students, and employees.

B. We do not engage in sexual or other harassment of supervisees, students, employees, research subjects, or colleagues.

C. All forms of sexual behavior, as defined in Principle III.G, with our supervisees, students, research subjects, and employees (except in employee situations involving domestic partners) are unethical.

D. We advise our students, supervisees, and employees against offering or engaging in, or holding themselves out as competent to engage in, professional services beyond their training, level of experience, and competence.

E. We do not harass or dismiss an employee who has acted in a reasonable, responsible, and ethical manner to protect, or intervene on behalf of, a client or other member of the public or another employee.

PRINCIPLE VI – INTERPROFESSIONAL RELATIONSHIPS

As members of AAPC, we relate to and cooperate with other professional persons in our community and beyond. We are part of a network of health care professionals and are expected to develop and maintain interdisciplinary and interprofessional relationships.

A. We do not offer ongoing clinical services to persons currently receiving treatment from another professional without prior knowledge of and in consultation with the other professional, with the clients' informed consent. Soliciting such clients is unethical.

B. We exercise care and interprofessional courtesy when approached for services by persons who claim or appear to have inappropriately terminated treatment with another professional.

PRINCIPLE VII – ADVERTISING

Any advertising by or for a member of AAPC, including announcements, public statements, and promotional activities, is undertaken with the purpose of helping the public make informed judgments and choices.

A. We do not misrepresent our professional qualifications, affiliations, and functions, or falsely imply sponsorship or certification by any organization.

B. We may use the following information to describe ourselves and the services we provide: name; highest relevant academic degree earned from an accredited institution; date, type, and level of certification or licensure; AAPC membership level, clearly stated; address and telephone number; office hours; a brief review of services offered, e.g., individual, couple, and group counseling; fee information; languages spoken; and policy regarding third party payments. Additional relevant information may be provided if it is legitimate, reasonable, free of deception, and not otherwise prohibited by these principles. We may not use the initials "AAPC" after our names in the manner of an academic degree.

C. Announcements and brochures promoting our services describe them with accuracy and dignity, devoid of all claims or evaluation. We may send them to professional persons, religious institutions, and other agencies, but to prospective individual clients only in response to inquires.

D. We do not make public statements which contain any of the following:

1. A false, fraudulent, misleading, deceptive, or unfair statement.

2. A misrepresentation of fact or a statement likely to mislead or deceive because in context it makes only a partial disclosure of relevant facts.

3. A testimonial from a client regarding the quality of services or products.

4. A statement intended or likely to create false or unjustified expectations of favorable results.

    5. A statement implying unusual, unique, or one-of-a-kind abilities, including misrepresentation through sensationalism, exaggeration, or superficiality.

    6. A statement intended or likely to exploit a client's fears, anxieties, or emotions.

    7. A statement concerning the comparative desirability of offered services.

    8. A statement of direct solicitation of individual clients.

E. We do not compensate in any way a representative of the press, radio, television, or other communication medium for the purpose of professional publicity and news items. A paid advertisement must be identified as such, unless it is contextually apparent that it is a paid advertisement. We are responsible for the content of such advertisement. An advertisement to the public by radio or television is to be prerecorded, approved by us, and a recording of the actual transmission retained in our possession.

F. Advertisements or announcements by us of workshops, clinics, seminars, growth groups, or similar services or endeavors, are to give a clear statement of purpose and a clear description of the experiences to be provided. The education, training, and experience of the provider(s) involved are to be appropriately specified.

G. Advertisements or announcements soliciting research participants, in which clinical or other professional services are offered as an inducement, make clear the nature of the services as well as the cost and other obligations or risks to be accepted by participants in the research.

CODE OF ETHICS PROCEDURES

(Amended April 28, 1994)

As members of the American Association of Pastoral Counselors, we are committed to accept the judgment of other members as to standards of professional ethics, subject to the procedures that follow. Refusal or failure to cooperate with an ethics investigation at any point may be considered grounds for Dismissal.

As members of AAPC, we are bound by ethical standards to take action, according to the procedures outlined herein, when it appears that another member has violated the Code of Ethics. Whenever ethical questions arise and the answers do not appear to be clear, we consult with the Regional Ethics Committee for information and clarification.

A. General Procedures (For "Sexual Misconduct Cases" see "E")

1. While all ethical violations are recognized as serious, if an alleged violation is not threatening to the well-being of the member or others, we are encouraged first to approach the member in question to see if the matter can be resolved through clarification or remonstrance.

2. If this fails, or if an alleged violation appears to be a serious threat to the well-being of the member or others, the matter is immediately referred to the Regional Ethics Committee. This constitutes a formal complaint and shall be made in writing to the Regional Ethics Committee, which begins an investigation as soon as possible and in a deliberate and careful manner.

3. If members receive complaints of unethical conduct against them, they shall promptly report the complaints to the Regional Ethics Committee.

4. Regional Ethics Committees shall consult with the Association Chair or Committee immediately upon receipt of a complaint. The Executive Director of AAPC shall be notified by phone of the complaint.

5. A Regional Ethics Committee begins an investigation as soon as a complaint from a primary party has been received. A copy of the complaint (or a summary or a portion of it which indicates the nature of the complaint) is sent to the member against whom it is directed.

6. A Regional Ethics Committee may also begin an investigation based upon information obtained from other sources, including but not limited to:

    a. Notification of Suspension or Dismissal from another professional organization or from the member's endorsing faith group.

b. The media.

c. Knowledge that a member has been convicted of, or is engaged in conduct which could lead to the conviction of, a felony or a misdemeanor related to the member's qualifications or functioning as a pastoral counselor.

d. Knowledge that a member has had a professional license or certificate suspended or revoked.

e. Knowledge that a member has shown a lack of competency to practice pastoral counseling due to impairment through physical or mental causes or the abuse of alcohol or other substances.

7. When a Regional Ethics Committee proceeds on its own initiative (in lieu of the receipt of a written complaint), it shall prepare a statement concerning the factual allegations against the member; a copy of this shall be sent to the member.

8. Complaints may be brought by anyone. Complaints by members shall be brought promptly, with due regard for client confidentiality.

9. Investigations usually include separate personal interviews by the Regional Ethics Committee with the person(s) who has made the complaint, with the member against whom the complaint has been made, and with anyone else deemed necessary to obtain needed information. All parties involved are to be supported while at the same time not given unnecessary information or promises.

10. Notes are to be kept which include dates and brief summaries of all phone calls and meetings. These notes are to be kept confidential, including the use of initials instead of names whenever feasible. These notes should be clear enough to enable a reasonable person to conclude that the Regional Committee's investigation was adequate and its findings sufficient to sustain its determination(s).

11. At the discretion of the Regional Ethics Chair, legal counsel may be obtained to ensure that these procedures are followed accurately. The member against whom a complaint has been made may

also seek legal counsel, at his/her own expense, but under no circumstances shall legal counsel be present at any Ethics Committee meeting or investigative interview.

12. Any member of a Regional Ethics Committee who has or has had a close personal or collegial relationship with the member under investigation shall be excused from the investigation and deliberations of that case. If this includes the chairperson, a chair pro-temp shall be named. Regional Ethics Committees may recruit any member(s) of AAPC, from any region, for a specific investigation.

13. Confidentiality is crucial. However, when it is deemed to be in the best interest of protecting the public and the Association and its members, if a Regional or Association Ethics Committee is approached by a member of AAPC or of the public and is asked about allegations against a particular member, the committee member or chairperson may reveal to that person that (a) an investigation of the alleged violation(s) is in process, or (b) that the member is under discipline, or either is or has been recommended for Dismissal. No other details are to be revealed.

14. Any member under investigation who moves to another region during the course of any disciplinary action shall notify in writing the Chairs of the Ethics Committees of both the former and new regions. A copy of each notification shall be sent to the other chairperson.

    a. Investigations shall be conducted and completed by the Ethics Committee of the region in which the alleged violation occurred.

    b. A copy of the complete file shall be sent to the Ethics Chair of the region into which the member relocates. That Chair shall be responsible for the management of the ongoing process until it is resolved in consultation with the original Ethics Chair.

    c. Responsibility for the management of the case shall be transferred to the Ethics Committee in the new region at a time that is deemed appropriate by both Regional Ethics Chairs.

15. Investigations can be held and disciplinary actions can be taken only against those who were members at the time the alleged

violation of the Code took place. Conversely, if a member resigns during or after such violation, or during the course of an investigation, ethics procedures shall proceed to completion.

B. Actions

When an investigation is complete, there are four courses of action that an Ethics Committee may take:

1. Advise that the complaint is unfounded.

2. Admonishment. This action is meant to be educational when a member has been unaware of having violated the Code of Ethics.

3. Reprimand. This action is a serious reproof or rebuke of the member. It is based upon an assessment that the member has accepted responsibility for the violation and that the reprimand is adequate to ensure that it will not reoccur.

Actions 2 and 3 may be taken only in those cases in which the violation is deemed not to be threatening to the well-being of the member or others. They are taken by the Regional Ethics Committees. The following is recommended by the Regional Ethics Committees for action by the Association Ethics Committee.

4. Dismissal. This action is taken when a violation of the Code is serious and demonstrates an essential lack of professional knowledge, procedures, and conduct, which are consistent with membership in AAPC.

    When deemed appropriate, the Association Ethics Committee, or a Board of Review on behalf of the Ethics Committee, may offer the member a voluntary reduction of membership level to a membership category which is more in keeping with the member's demonstrated level of pastoral functioning and need for supervision. The member is subsequently allowed to advance in membership categories through normal Membership Committee procedures; i.e., reattain required number of hours of supervision for advancement, reappear before Membership Committee, etc.

    When dismissed, and at the conclusion of possible appeals, the member shall submit membership certificate to the Executive

Director. When a voluntary reduction of membership category has been accepted, the member shall submit existing membership certificate and may request a certificate for the new membership category at own expense.

The action of Dismissal may be taken in any case but is mandated when a member has been found guilty in a court of law of a felony, or of a misdemeanor which is related to the member's functioning as a pastoral counselor.

C. Appeals Process and Records

With each of the four actions above, the action is communicated to the complainant and to the member by certified mail, return receipt requested, with notification that the decision may be appealed.

1. Actions 2 and 3 may be appealed to the Association Ethics Committee, at which point the Regional Ethics Chair forwards the complete file along with a summary of the case to the Association Ethics Chair.

    a. The Association Ethics Chair decides upon and organizes any additional investigation that may be necessary.

    b. When this is accomplished, the Association Ethics Committee reviews the case and meets either in person or by conference call to discuss the appeal and to reach a decision.

    c. If no appeal is received within 30 days of this receipt, a chronological summary (without names) of the case is sealed in an envelope with only the member's name on the outside. It is then sent to the Executive Director of AAPC for safe keeping.

    d. The summary is to be kept by the Executive Director of AAPC for a period of twenty years, or longer if another investigation is begun. In the event another investigation of that member begins, the summary may be sent upon request to a Regional or Association Ethics Committee.

2. Action 4 may be appealed to an Appeal Board through notification of the Association Chair. The Appeal Board shall be made up of the Chair of the Association Ethics Committee, the Vice President

of AAPC, and a member-at-large in AAPC, chosen by the Association Ethics Chair. The Religious Endorsing Body (REB) representative shall be invited to participate as an observing (non-voting) member of the Appeal Board. The REB representative shall be informed of the details of a case only should they choose to participate on the Board. The Appeal Board may also include a representative of the AAPC Executive Director as a non-voting, observing member.

a. The Association Ethics Chair, in consultation with legal counsel, decides upon and organizes any additional investigation that may be necessary.

b. When this is accomplished, the Appeal Board shall review the case and meet either in person or by conference call to discuss the appeal. It then reaches a final decision about the appeal.

c. If no appeal is received within 30 days of the above mentioned receipt, the procedure is the same as in 1.c.

d. The file, with summary, shall be kept by the Executive Director of AAPC indefinitely and shall be destroyed one year after the Association learns of the member's death. A Regional or Association Ethics Committee may request this file if another complaint is received or investigation is begun regarding the member. In addition, in the case of Dismissal, the file shall also be sent upon request to a Regional or Association Membership Committee if the person reapplies for membership.

e. If a member appeals a decision for Dismissal, the member shall cease all functioning as a pastoral counselor during the appeal.

3. Decisions by the Appeal Board regarding appeals are final.

D. Notifications

1. When issued a Reprimand, the member shall report this status in writing to a present or prospective employer, including supervisors and consultants, and copies shall be sent to the Regional Ethics Chair. Notifications of a Reprimand shall be sent by the Association Ethics Chair to the member's endorsing faith group, relevant state regulatory agencies, and any and all other professional organizations to which the member belongs.

2. Determinations of Reprimand or Dismissal, once the appeal time or procedures are over, are publicized to the membership in the next AAPC Newsletter. The announcement is limited to the member's full name and highest earned degree, geographical location, the fact and date of Reprimand or Dismissal, and the specific Principle(s) of the Code violated. If a member is dismissed for violation of Principle VIII, first paragraph (refusal or failure to cooperate with an ethics investigation at any point), all other Principles alleged to have been violated shall also be listed.

3. In the case of Dismissal, the Association Ethics Chair, once the appeal time or procedures are over, shall notify the member's endorsing faith group, relevant state regulatory agencies, and any and all other professional organizations to which the member belongs. The specific information communicated is the same as above.

E. Sexual Misconduct Cases

When a complaint is received alleging sexual misconduct or violative harassment of Principle III. G and H, the following procedures shall pertain:

1. Upon receipt of a complaint, or information of a potential complaint, the Regional Ethics Chair shall immediately contact the AAPC Executive Director and the Association Ethics Chair to advise them of all initial information received, forwarding to the Executive Director a completed Regional Ethics Committee special report form on the matter. An investigatory process shall commence under the direct guidance of the Association's legal counsel, utilizing regional ethics committee members and resources as needed.

2. The Association Ethics Chair shall appoint a three member subcommittee of Association Committee members to receive the results of the investigation and act as a Board of Review for the case. The Regional Ethics Chair of the region from which the complaint arose shall be a member of the subcommittee, barring conflicts, and will not act as a chair. Only members of the Association Ethics Committee may serve on the Board of Review. However, as a matter of discretion, the Association Ethics Chair may appoint to review boards a qualified fourth member in order to attain gender, racial, cultural, faith group, or sexual orientation

balance and fairness. This person may be from the membership of AAPC, or, as deemed necessary, from the general public.

3. When acting as a Board of Review, the subcommittee shall act on behalf of the Association Ethics Committee, review results of the investigations, make provisions as necessary for further fact finding, and reach a decision on a disposition of the matter in accordance with Procedures, B.1-4. The deliberations of the Board of Review are held in executive session and upon invitation open to the member, the complainant, and their respective counsel. Investigations, deliberation of facts, conclusions, and any disciplinary actions are not intended to replicate a court of law or legal process. Reasonableness and fairness shall be the standard for the Ethics Committee press rather than strict adherence to legal rules of evidence used in court.

4. The decision of the Board of Review may be appealed by the member only when the decision involves Reprimand or Dismissal. Appeals are made to an Appeal Board, as outlined in Section C.2 (above), which has final jurisdiction. Appeals must be made within 30 days of notification of the Board of Review's findings. If litigation is pending, the Board of Review may defer its decision to the outcome of such litigation, and on an interim basis, impose nonappealable terms or conditions of discipline. If new and material facts are discovered within 30 days of the decision of the Board of Review, the member or complainant may ask the Board of Review for a re-hearing, provided that no appeal has been previously taken. A re-hearing is at the sole discretion of the Board of Review.

F. Board of Emergency Review

1. To protect the public welfare, the rights of AAPC members, and the interest of the Association, a Board of Emergency Review is established. This board consists of the President (ex-officio), the Vice President, the Secretary, the Executive Director, the Deputy Executive Director, and at least one AAPC Committee Chair of a relevant committee or his/her designee. The Board of Emergency Review shall have legal counsel present whenever action is to be taken.

2. Upon notification that a member's conduct and actions appear to be so egregious that waiting for action and decision through the normal committee process presents an unacceptable level or risk to the public, the member, or the Association, the Board of Emergency Review has the authority to meet, to consider the facts, and to temporarily withdraw membership credentials pending full investigation of the case.

3. Notification shall be made to the member in writing. Further, notification shall be made to the committee investigating the case. The committee shall be notified that the Board of Emergency Review's decision to temporarily withdraw the member's credentials does not constitute a finding of guilt on the charges under investigation and does not absolve the committee of its responsibility to fully investigate the charges, render a decision, and make ultimate disposition of the case.

4. Notification shall be made to outside authorities, i.e., endorsing bodies, licensing boards, and other professional organizations to which the member belongs. These bodies will be notified in writing and told that the decision of the Board of Emergency Review does not constitute a finding of guilt on any charges but was taken only to protect the interest of the public, the member, and/or the AAPC.

Appendix C

Multiaxial Evaluation Report Form

The following is offered as one possible form for reporting multiaxial evaluations. In some settings, this form may be used exactly as is; in other settings, the form may be adapted to satisfy special needs.

AXIS I: CLINICAL SYNDROMES

OTHER CONDITIONS THAT MAY BE A FOCUS OF CLINICAL ATTENTION

DSM-IV Code   DSM-IV Name

— — — - — —   _____

— — — - — —   _____

— — — - — —   _____

AXIS II: PERSONALITY DISORDERS

DSM-IV Code   DSM-IV Name

— — — - — —   _____

— — — - — —   _____

AXIS III: GENERAL MEDICAL CONDITIONS

ICD-9-CM Code   ICD-9-CM Name

— — — - — —   _____

— — — - — —   _____

— — — - — —   _____

AXIS IV: PSYCHOLOGICAL AND ENVIRONMENTAL PROBLEMS

Check:

_____ Problems with primary support group (Childhood [V61.9], Adult

      [V61.9], Parent–Child [V61.2]). Specify: _____

_____ Problems related to the social environment (V62.4).

      Specify: _____

_____ Educational problem (V62.3). Specify: _____

_____ Occupational problem (V62.2). Specify: _____

_____ Housing problem (V60.9). Specify: _____

_____ Economic problem (V60.9). Specify: _____

_____ Problems with access to health care services (V63.9).

      Specify: _____

_____ Problems related to interaction with the legal system/crime

      (V62.5). Specify: _____

_____ Other psychosocial problem (V62.9). Specify: _____

AXIS V: GLOBAL ASSESSMENT OF FUNCTIONING SCALE
        Code: ___ ___

Reprinted with permission from the *Diagnostic and Statistical Manual of Mental Disorders,* Fourth Edition, Washington, DC, American Psychiatric Association, 1994.

Appendix D

Global Assessment
of Functioning (GAF) Scale

Consider psychological, social, and occupational functioning on a hypothetical continuum of mental health/illness. Do not include impairment in functioning due to physical (or environmental) limitations.

Code (**Note:** Use intermediate codes when appropriate, e.g., 45, 68, 72.)

100   **Superior functioning in a wide range of activities, life's problems never seem to get out of hand, is sought out by others**
91   **because of his or her many positive qualities. No symptoms.**

90   **Absent or minimal symptoms** (e.g., mild anxiety before an exam), **good functioning in all areas, interested and involved in a wide range of activities, socially effective, generally satisfied with life, no more than everyday problems or concerns** (e.g., an occasional
81   argument with family members).

80   **If symptoms are present, they are transient and expectable reactions to psychosocial stressors** (e.g., difficulty concentrating after family argument); **no more than slight impairment in social, occupational, or school functioning** (e.g., temporarily falling
71   behind in schoolwork).

70   **Some mild symptoms** (e.g., depressed mood and mild insomnia) **OR some difficulty in social, occupational, or school functioning** (e.g., occasional truancy, or theft within the household), **but generally functioning pretty well, has some meaningful interpersonal**
61   **relationships.**

60   **Moderate symptoms** (e.g., flat affect and circumstantial speech, occasional panic attacks) **OR moderate difficulty in social, occupa-**

| tional, or school functioning (e.g, few friends, conflicts with peers
51   or co-workers).

50   Serious symptoms (e.g., suicidal ideation, several obsessional rituals,
| frequent shoplifting) OR any serious impairment in social, occupa-
41   tional, or school functioning (e.g., no friends, unable to keep a job).

40   Some impairment in reality testing or communication (e.g.,
| speech is at times illogical, obscure, or irrelevant) OR major impair-
| ment in several areas, such as work or school, family relations,
| judgment, thinking, or mood (e.g., depressed man avoids friends,
| neglects family, and is unable to work; child frequently beats up
31   younger children, is defiant at home, and is failing at school).

30   Behavior is considerably influenced by delusions or hallucinations
| OR serious impairment in communication or judgment (e.g.,
| sometimes incoherent, acts grossly inappropriately, suicidal pre-
| occupation) OR inability to function in almost all areas (e.g., stays
21   in bed all day; no job, home, or friends).

20   Some danger of hurting self or others (e.g., suicide attempts with-
| out clear expectation of death; frequently violent; manic excitement)
| OR gross impairment in communication (e.g., largely incoherent
11   or mute).

10   Persistent danger of severely hurting self or others (e.g., recurrent
| violence) OR persistent inability to maintain minimal personal
1   hygiene OR serious suicidal act with clear expectation of death.

0   Inadequate information.

    The ratings of overall psychological functioning on a scale of 0-100 was
operationalized by Luborsky in the Health-Sickness Rating Scale (Luborsky, L.,
"Clinicians' Judgments of Mental Health." *Archives of General Psychiatry*
7:407-417, 1962). Spitzer and colleagues developed a revision of the Health-Sickness Rating Scale called the Global Assessment Scale (GAS) (Endicott, J., Spitzer, R.L., Fleiss, J.L., and Cohen, J., "The Global Assessment Scale: A Procedure
for Measuring Overall Severity of Psychiatric Disturbance." *Archives of General
Psychiatry* 33:766-771, 1976). A modified version of the GAS was included in
DSM-III-R as the Global Assessment of Functioning (GAF) Scale. Ibid., p. 32.

References

Preface

1. Petruska Clarkson, "Integrative Psychotherapy, Integrating Psychotherapies, or Psychotherapy after 'Schoolism'?" In Colin Feltham (ed.), *Which Psychotherapy?* Thousand Oaks, CA: Sage, 1997, p. 37.

Introduction

1. Cf. E. Brooks Holifield, *A History of Pastoral Care in America* (Nashville: Abingdon Press, 1983), and John T. McNeill, *A History of the Cure of Souls* (New York: Harper Brothers, 1951).

2. Joint Commission of Mental Illness and Health, *Action for Mental Health* (New York: Basic Books, 1961), 103.

3. I. Elinson, E. Padilla, and M. Perkins, *Public Image of Mental Health Services* (New York: Mental Health Materials Center, 1967).

4. Joseph Veroff, Richard A. Kulka, and Elizabeth Douvan, *Mental Health in America: Patterns of Seeking Help from 1957 to 1976* (New York: Basic Books, 1981).

5. J. McHolland, ed., *The Future of Pastoral Counseling* (Fairfax, VA: AAPC, 1993), 115.

6. Jerome D. Frank, The Demoralized Mind, *Psychology Today* 6 (April 1973), 26.

7. Helen Harris Perlman, *Relationship: The Heart of Helping People* (Chicago: University of Chicago Press, 1979), 12.

8. Petruska Clarkson, "Integrative Psychotherapy, Integrating Psychotherapies, or Psychotherapy after 'Schoolism'?" In Colin Feltham (ed.), *Which Psychotherapy?* Thousand Oaks, CA: Sage, 1997, p. 35.

9. William U. Snyder and June B. Snyder, *The Psychotherapy Relationship* (New York: Macmillan, 1961), 287.

10. Ibid., 270.

11. Joseph W. Eaton, The Client-Practitioner Relationship as a Variable in the Evaluation of Treatment Outcome, *Psychiatry* 22 (May 1959), 189-195.

12. Donald M. Sundland and Edwin N. Barker, The Orientations of Psychotherapists, *Journal of Consulting Psychology* 4 (April 1962), 201-212.

13. F. E. Fiedler, A Comparison of Therapeutic Relationship in Psychoanalytic, Nondirective, and Adlerian Therapy, *Journal of Consulting Psychology* 14 (December 1950), 436-445.

PART I

1. Eli A. Rubenstein and Morris B. Parloff, eds., *Research in Psychotherapy* (Washington: American Psychological Association, 1959), 235.

Chapter 1

1. Dayton G. Van Deusen, *Redemptive Counseling* (Richmond, VA: John Knox Press, 1960), 79.

2. C. H. Patterson, *Relationship Counseling and Psychotherapy* (New York: Harper and Row, 1974), 11.

3. Charles V. Gerkin, *The Living Human Document: Re-Visioning Pastoral Counseling in a Hermeneutical Mode* (Nashville: Abingdon, 1984), 145.

4. Otto Rank, *Will Therapy and Truth and Reality,* translated by Jessie Taft (New York: Alfred A. Knopf, 1945).

5. Martin Buber, *I and Thou,* translated by Walter Kaufman and G. S. Smith (New York: Scribner's, 1970).

6. Scripture quotations in this book are taken from the New Revised Standard Version, 1989.

7. Abraham Maslow, *Motivation and Personality,* second edition (New York: Harper and Row, 1970).

8. Paul E. Johnson, *Psychology of Pastoral Care* (Nashville: Abingdon, 1953), 29.

9. Seward Hiltner, *Theological Dynamics* (Nashville: Abingdon, 1972), 18-35.

10. Johnson, *Psychology of Pastoral Care,* 30.

11. Frederick C. Thorne, *Principles of Personality Counseling* (Brandon, VT: Journal of Clinical Psychology, 1950), 22.

12. Robert A. Harper, *Psychoanalysis and Psychotherapy: 36 Systems* (New York: Jason Aronson, 1974).

13. Richie Herink, ed., *The Psychology Handbook* (New York: New American Library, 1980).

14. Patterson, *Relationship Counseling and Psychotherapy,* 9; Patterson, C. H. The Therapeutic Relationship: Foundations for an Eclectic Psychotherapy (Monterey, CA: Brooks/Cole, 1986).

15. William B. Oglesby, Jr., *Biblical Themes for Pastoral Care* (Nashville: Abingdon, 1980), 13-32.

16. J. Harold Ellens, *God's Grace and Human Health* (Nashville: Abingdon, 1982), 114.

17. D. Smith, Trends in Counseling and Psychotherapy, *American Psychologist* 37 (1982).

18. Cf. bibliography. The volumes wherein these authors state their eclectic positions are all listed in the bibliography.

19. Wayne E. Oates, *Protestant Pastoral Counseling* (Philadelphia: Westminster, 1962), 190-91, 212.

20. C. W. Brister, *Pastoral Care in the Church* (New York: Harper, 1964), 170.

21. Edgar N. Jackson, *The Pastor and His People* (Manhasset, NY: Channel, 1963), 133.

22. F. Fiedler, "A Comparative Investigation of Early Therapeutic Relationships" (PhD Diss., University of Chicago, 1949).

23. Ralph William Heine, "An Investigation of the Relationship Between Change and the Responsible Factors as Seen by Psychotherapists of the Psychoanalytic, Adlerian, and Nondirective Schools" (PhD Diss., University of Chicago, 1950).

24. John D. Black, Common Factors of the Patient-Therapist Relationship in Diverse Psychotherapies, *Journal of Clinical Psychology* 8 (July 1952), 302-306.

25. Oliver Hutchings Bown, "An Investigation of Therapeutic Relationships in Client-Centered Psychotherapy" (PhD Diss., University of Chicago, 1954).

26. Albert Ellis, "The Future of Cognitive-Behavior and Rational Emotive Behavior Therapy." In Stephen Palmer and Ved Varma, eds., *The Future of Counseling and Psychotherapy*, Thousand Oaks, CA: Sage, 1997, p. 1.

27. J. C. Norcross, ed., *Handbook of Eclectic Psychotherapy* (New York: Brunner/Mazel, 1986).

28. Richard Dayringer, ed., *Dealing with Depression: Five Pastoral Interventions* (Binghamton, NY: The Haworth Press, 1995).

29. Wayne E. Oates, ed., *An Introduction to Pastoral Counseling* (Nashville: Broadman, 1959), 5.

30. Jackson, *The Pastor and His People,* 19-20.

31. Everett Barnard, You and Your Relationship, *Church Administration* 9 (November 1967), 12.

32. Paul E. Johnson, *Psychology of Religion* (Nashville: Abingdon, 1959), 69-70.

33. Charles Stewart, Relationship Counseling, *Journal of Pastoral Care* 13 (Winter 1959), 218.

34. Van Deusen, *Redemptive Counseling,* 80.

35. Edward E. Thornton, *Theology and Pastoral Counseling* (Englewood Cliffs, NJ: Prentice-Hall, 1964), 40, 71.

36. Oates, *Protestant Pastoral Counseling,* 57-58.

Chapter 2

1. Seward Hiltner and Lowell G. Colston, *The Context of Pastoral Counseling* (Nashville: Abingdon, 1961), 27.

2. Ronald R. Lee, *Clergy and Clients: The Practice of Pastoral Psychotherapy* (New York: Seabury, 1980), and Carroll A. Wise, *Pastoral Psychotherapy* (New York: Jason Aronson, 1983).

3. Lawrence M. Brammer and Everett L. Shostrom, *Therapeutic Psychology* (Englewood Cliffs, NJ: Prentice-Hall, 1968), 144.

4. John Patton, *Pastoral Counseling: A Ministry of the Church* (Nashville: Abingdon, 1983), 167.

5. Carl R. Rogers, *Counseling and Psychotherapy* (Boston: Houghton Mifflin, 1942), 30.

6. Helen Harris Perlman, *Relationship: The Heart of Helping People* (Chicago: University of Chicago Press, 1979), 22-47.

7. Sheldon Cashdan, *Object Relations Therapy: Using the Relationship* (New York: W. W. Norton, 1988), xii.

8. Michael Kahn, *Between Therapist and Client: The New Relationship,* revised edition (New York: Freeman, 1997), 112.

9. Carl R. Rogers, ed., *The Therapeutic Relationship and Its Impact* (Westport, CT: Greenwood, 1967), 81-82.

10. Carl Gustav Jung, *The Practice of Psychotherapy,* edited by H. Read, M. Fordham, and G. Adler, 16 vols. (New York: Pantheon, 1953-1961), 137.

11. Otto Rank, *Will Therapy and Truth and Reality,* translated by Jessie Taft (New York: Alfred A. Knopf, 1945), 37.

12. Rogers, *Counseling and Psychotherapy,* 29.

13. C. J. Gelso and J. A. Carter, The Relationship in Counseling and Psychotherapy: Components, Consequences, and Theoretical Antecedents, *The Counseling Psychologist, 13,* 155-243, 1985; M. J. Lambert, D. A. Shapiro, and A. E. Bergin, The Effectiveness of Psychotherapy. In S. L. Garfield and A. E. Bergin, eds., *Handbook of Psychotherapy and Behavior Change*, third edition, New York: Wiley, 1986, pp. 157-211; D. E. Orlinsky and K. I. Howard, Process and Outcome in Psychotherapy, Ibid., pp. 311-381.

14. Arthur H. Becker, "The Function of Relationship in Pastoral Counseling" (PhD Diss., Boston University, 1958), abstract.

15. F. E. Fiedler, The Concept of an Ideal Therapeutic Relationship, *Journal of Consulting Psychology* 14 (August 1950), 239-245.

16. Becker, "The Function of Relationship in Pastoral Counseling," 298-308.

17. I. V. Coleman, Patient-Physician Relationships in Psychotherapy, *American Journal of Psychiatry* 104 (April, 1948), 641.

18. Wayne E. Oates, ed., *An Introduction to Pastoral Counseling* (Nashville: Broadman, 1959), 75.

19. Brammer and Shostrom, *Therapeutic Psychology,* 145-149.

20. Fiedler, The Concept of an Ideal Therapeutic Relationship, 241.

21. Becker, "The Function of Relationship in Pastoral Counseling," 250, 253, 285.

22. William Schofield, *Psychotherapy: The Purchase of Friendship* (Englewood Cliffs, NJ: Prentice-Hall, 1964), 89.

23. Becker, "The Function of Relationship in Pastoral Counseling," 387-88.

24. Howard Clinebell, *Basic Types of Pastoral Care and Counseling,* revised edition (Nashville: Abingdon, 1984), 378.

25. William U. Snyder and June B. Snyder, *The Psychotherapy Relationship* (New York: Macmillan, 1961), 165.

26. Richard E. Farson, Introjection in the Psychotherapeutic Relationship, *Journal of Consulting Psychology* 8 (Winter 1961), 341.

27. American Association of Pastoral Counselors, *Handbook* (Fairfax, VA: American Association of Pastoral Counselors, 1986), 2:2.

28. I. D. Yalom. *Existential Psychotherapy.* (New York: Basic Books, 1980), p. 401.

29. Carroll A. Wise, *Pastoral Counseling: Its Theory and Practice* (New York: Harper Brothers, 1951), 39.

30. Edgar N. Jackson, *The Pastor and His People* (Manhasset, NY: Channel, 1963), 18.

31. Morris B. Parloff, Some Factors Affecting the Quality of Therapeutic Relationships, *Journal of Abnormal and Social Psychology* 52 (January 1956), 5-10.

32. Becker, "The Function of Relationship in Pastoral Counseling," 269.

33. Carl R. Rogers, *The Clinical Treatment of the Problem Child* (New York: Houghton Mifflin, 1939), 284.

34. Jerome D. Frank, The Dynamics of the Psychotherapeutic Relationship, *Psychiatry* 22 (February 1959), 17-29.

35. William Doherty, *Soul Searching: Why Psychotherapy Must Promote Moral Responsibility* (New York: Basic, 1995).

36. Irene E. Waskow, Counselor Attitudes and Client Behavior, *Journal of Consulting Psychology* 27 (October 1963), 409.

37. C. W. Brister, *Pastoral Care in the Church* (New York: Harper and Row, 1964).

38. Carl R. Rogers, *On Becoming a Person* (Boston: Houghton Mifflin, 1961), 330.

39. Karl Menninger and Philip S. Holzman, *Theory of Psychoanalytic Technique,* second edition (New York: Basic Books, 1973), 96.

40. Rogers, *On Becoming a Person,* 50-55.

41. Joint Commission of Mental Illness and Health, *Action for Mental Health* (New York: Basic Books, 1961), 103.

42. Martin G. Vorhaus, *The Changing Patient-Doctor Relationship* (New York: Horizon, 1957), 23.

43. Wayne E. Oates, ed., *The Findings of the Commission on the Ministry, Annals of the New York Academy of Sciences* 63 (November 1955), 416-417.

44. Richard Dayringer, A Learning Theory Approach to Pastoral Counseling, *Pastoral Psychology* 20 (March 1969), 40.

45. Snyder and Snyder, *The Psychotherapy Relationship,* 149.

46. Petruska Clarkson, "Integrative Psychotherapy, Integrating Psychotherapies, or Psychotherapy after 'Schoolism'?" In Colin Feltham, ed., *Which Psychotherapy?* (Thousand Oaks, CA: Sage, 1997), p. 35.

47. Stanley W. Standal and Raymond J. Corsini, eds., *Critical Incidents in Psychotherapy* (Englewood Cliffs, NJ: Prentice-Hall, 1959), 94.

48. Frederick C. Thorne, *Principles of Personality Counseling* (Brandon, VT: Journal of Clinical Psychology, 1950), 127.

49. Rogers, *On Becoming a Person,* 43.

50. Thorne, *Principles of Personality Counseling,* 155-156.

51. Wayne E. Oates, *The Christian Pastor* (Philadelphia: Westminster, 1964), 145.

52. Jackson, *The Pastor and His People,* 144.

53. Richard Dayringer, Relationships—The Chaplain's Basic Tool, *American Protestant Hospital Association Bulletin* 30 (January 1967), 11, 23-28.

54. Seward Hiltner, *Pastoral Counseling* (Nashville: Abingdon, 1949), 21.

55. Hiltner and Colston, *The Context of Pastoral Counseling,* 21.

PART II

1. Otto Rank, *Will Therapy and Truth and Reality,* translated by Jessie Taft (New York: Alfred A. Knopf, 1945), 167-169.

Chapter 3

1. Lawrence M. Brammer and Everett L. Shostrom, *Therapeutic Psychology* (Englewood Cliffs, NJ: Prentice-Hall, 1968), 171.

2. Carroll A. Wise, *Pastoral Counseling: Its Theory and Practice* (New York: Harper Brothers, 1951), 40.

3. Arnold Buchheimer and Sarah Carter Balogh, *The Counseling Relationship: A Casebook* (Chicago: Science Research Associates, 1961), 4.

4. Glenn V. Ramsey, The Initial Counseling Interview, *Pastoral Psychology* 17 (November 1966), 30.

5. Rollo May, *The Art of Counseling* (New York: Abingdon-Cokesbury, 1939), 127-129.

6. Richard Dayringer, The Problem-Oriented Record in Pastoral Counseling, *Religion and Health* 17 (1978), 39-47.

7. Paul Pruyser, *The Minister as Diagnostician: Personal Problems in Pastoral Perspective* (Philadelphia: Westminster, 1976).

8. R. F. Larson, The Clergyman's Role in the Therapeutic Process: Disagreement Between Clergymen and Psychiatrists, *Psychiatry* 31 (1968), 250-263.

9. Edgar Draper, *Psychiatry and Pastoral Care* (Englewood Cliffs, NJ: Prentice-Hall, 1965), 31.

10. Ramsey, The Initial Counseling Interview, 33.

11. Seward Hiltner and Lowell G. Colston, *The Context of Pastoral Counseling* (Nashville: Abingdon, 1961), 55-56.

12. Draper, *Psychiatry and Pastoral Care,* 66-68, 115.

13. Oscar Pfister, *Christianity and Fear* (London: George Allen and Unwin, 1948), 552.

14. American Pyschiatric Association, *Diagnostic and Statistical Manual of Mental Disorders*—fourth edition (New York: American Psychiatric Association, 1994).

15. Carl R. Rogers, *Counseling and Psychotherapy* (Boston: Houghton Mifflin, 1942), 250-251.

16. Brammer and Shostrom, *Therapeutic Psychology,* 183.

17. William F. May, Code, Covenant, Contract, or Philanthropy, *Hastings Center Report* 5 (December 1975), 29-38; *The Physician's Convenant: Images of the Healer in Medical Ethics* (Philadelphia: Westminster, 1983).

18. Richard E. Farson, Introjection in the Psychotherapeutic Relationship, *Journal of Consulting Psychology* 8 (Winter 1961), 279.

19. Wayne E. Oates, *Protestant Pastoral Counseling* (Philadelphia: Westminster, 1962), 107.

Chapter 4

1. Charles William Stewart, *The Minister as Marriage Counselor,* revised edition (New York: Abingdon, 1970), 37.

2. Ibid., 35.

3. C. W. Brister, *Pastoral Care in the Church,* third edition (New York: Harper and Row, 1992), 201.

4. Wayne E. Oates, *The Christian Pastor* (Philadelphia: Westminster, 1964), 69-91.

5. Don S. Browning, *The Moral Context of Pastoral Care* (Philadelphia: Westminster, 1976).

6. Seward Hiltner, *Pastoral Counseling* (Nashville: Abingdon, 1949), 150.

7. Brister, *Pastoral Care in the Church,* third edition (New York: Harper and Row, 1992), 97.

8. Wayne E. Oates, *Protestant Pastoral Counseling* (Philadelphia: Westminster, 1962), 143.

9. Rollo May, *The Art of Counseling,* revised edition (New York: Gardner Press, 1989), 128-129.

10. John Levy, Relationship Therapy, *American Journal of Orthopsychiatry* 8 (January 1938), 65.

11. Heinz L. Ansbacher and Rowena R. Ansbacher, *The Individual Psychology of Alfred Adler* (New York: Basic Books, 1956), 339.

12. Harry Stack Sullivan, *The Psychiatric Interview,* edited by Helen Swick Perry and Mary Ladd Gawel (New York: W. W. Norton, 1954), 28.

Chapter 5

1. Carroll A. Wise, *Pastoral Counseling: Its Theory and Practice* (New York: Harper Brothers, 1951), 40.

2. Lawrence M. Brammer and Everett L. Shostrom, *Therapeutic Psychology* (Englewood Cliffs, NJ: Prentice-Hall, 1968), 94.

3. Arthur H. Becker, "The Function of Relationship in Pastoral Counseling" (PhD Diss., Boston University, 1958), 389.

4. Ibid., 373-374.

5. C. B. Truax and Robert R. Carkhuff, *Toward Effective Counseling and Psychotherapy: Training and Practice* (Chicago: Adeline, 1967).

6. Leona E. Tyler, *The Work of the Counselor* (New York: Appleton-Century-Crofts, 1953), 289.

7. Bernard G. Berenson and Robert R. Carkhuff, *Sources of Gain in Counseling and Psychotherapy* (New York: Holt, Rinehart and Winston, 1967); Robert R. Carkhuff, *Helping and Human Relations: A Primer for Lay and Professional Helpers,* volume 1, *Selection and Training,* and volume 2, *Practice and Research* (New York: Holt, Rinehart and Winston, 1969); Robert R. Carkhuff and Bernard G. Berenson, *Beyond Counseling and Therapy* (New York: Holt, Rinehart and Winston, 1967); and Truax and Carkhuff, *Toward Effective Counseling and Psychotherapy* (Chicago: Adeline, 1967).

8. C. H. Patterson, *Relationship Counseling and Psychotherapy* (New York: Harper and Row, 1974), 49-96.

9. Eugene W. Kelly, Jr., *Relationship-Centered Counseling* (New York: Springer, 1994), 180.

10. Carl R. Rogers, *On Becoming a Person* (Boston: Houghton Mifflin, 1961), 18.

11. Robert Dean Quinn, "Psychotherapists' Expressions as an Index to the Quality of Early Therapeutic Relationships Established by Representatives of the Nondirective, Adlerian and Psychoanalytic Schools" (PhD Diss., University of Chicago).

12. Paul E. Johnson, *Person and Counselor* (Nashville: Abingdon, 1967), 175-176.

13. James E. Dittes, Galvanic Skin Response as a Measure of Patient's Reaction to Therapist's Permissiveness, *Journal of Abnormal Psychology* 55 (November 1957), 302-303.

14. Carkhuff and Berenson, *Beyond Counseling and Therapy,* 29.

15. Ibid., 30.

16. William U. Snyder and June B. Snyder, *The Psychotherapy Relationship* (New York: Macmillan, 1961), 351.

17. Eugene W. Kelly, Jr., *Relationship-Centered Counseling* (New York: Springer, 1994), 191

18. Jessie Taft, *The Dynamics of Therapy in a Controlled Relationship* (New York: Macmillan, 1933), 118.

19. David Augsburger, *Caring Enough to Confront* (Ventura, CA: Regal, 1980).

20. Carkhuff, *Helping and Human Relations,* 1:191.

21. Ibid., 2:93.

22. Ralph L. Underwood, *Empathy and Confrontation in Pastoral Care* (Philadelphia: Fortress, 1985), 112,113.

23. Ibid., 1:208-209.

24. Snyder and Snyder, *The Psychotherapy Relationship,* 257.

25. Caryl T. Moy, "Touch in the Therapeutic Relationship: An Exploratory Study with Therapists Who Touch" (PhD Diss., Southern Illinois University, 1980), and J. M. Wilson, The Value of Touch in Psychotherapy, *American Journal of Orthopsychiatry* 52(1) (1982); Zachary Thomas, *Healting Touch: The Church's Forgotten Language* (Louisville: Westminister of John Knox, 1994).

26. Patterson, *Relationship Counseling and Psychotherapy,* 83-89.

27. Snyder and Snyder, *The Psychotherapy Relationship,* 345.

28. Carkhuff, *Helping and Human Relations,* 1:212.

29. Snyder and Snyder, *The Psychotherapy Relationship,* 291-350.

30. Lewis R. Wolberg, *The Technique of Psychotherapy* (New York: Grune and Stratton, 1954), 499-503.

31. Rogers, *On Becoming a Person,* 16-17.

32. Mudd and Krich, *Man and Wife,* 236-41.

33. Jerome D. Frank, *Persuasion and Healing: A Comparative Study of Psychotherapy,* revised edition (Baltimore: Johns Hopkins Press, 1973), 168.

34. Carroll A. Wise, *Pastoral Psychotherapy* (New York: Jason Aronson, 1983), 197.

Chapter 6

1. Peter D. Blanck, *Nonverbal Communication in the Clinical Context* (University Park: Pennsylvania State University Press, 1986); Peter Bull, *Body Movement and Interpersonal Communication* (New York: John Wiley and Sons, 1983); Loretta Malandro, *Nonverbal Communication* (New York: Random House, 1988).

2. Rollo May, *The Art of Counseling,* revised edition (New York: Gardner, 1989), 84.

3. Ibid., 107.

4. Theodore Reik, *Listening With the Third Ear* (New York: Grove, 1948), 157-158.

5. Wayne E. Oates, *The Christian Pastor* (Philadelphia: Westminster, 1964), 241-245.

6. Gaylord Noyce, *The Art of Pastoral Counseling* (Atlanta: John Knox, 1981), 43, 50.

7. Oates, *The Christian Pastor,* 245.

Chapter 7

1. Carl R. Rogers, *On Becoming a Person* (Boston: Houghton Mifflin, 1961), 345.

2. Arthur H. Becker, "The Function of Relationship in Pastoral Counseling" (PhD Diss., Boston University, 1958), 264.

3. Wayne E. Oates, *Protestant Pastoral Counseling* (Philadelphia: Westminster, 1962), 175-177.

4. Lawrence M. Brammer and Everett L. Shostrom, *Therapeutic Psychology* (Englewood Cliffs, NJ: Prentice-Hall, 1968), 175.

5. C. W. Brister, *Pastoral Care in the Church,* third edition (New York: Harper and Row, 1992), 194.

Chapter 8

1. Robert Jean Campbell, *Psychiatric Dictionary,* fifth edition (New York: Oxford University Press, 1981), 518.

2. Carl R. Rogers, *Counseling and Psychotherapy* (Boston: Houghton Mifflin, 1942), 241.

3. Sigmund Freud, *The Standard Edition of the Complete Psychological Works of Sigmund Freud,* translated and edited by James Strachey, 24 volumes (London: Hogarth, 1955-1961), 12:104.

4. Ibid., 12:105.

5. E. Wesley Hiler, An Analysis of Patient-Therapist Compatibility, *Journal of Consulting Psychology* 23 (October 1958), 346.

6. Kenneth Heller and Arnold P. Goldstein, Client Dependency and Therapist Expectancy as Relationship Maintaining Variables in Psychotherapy, *Journal of Consulting Psychology* 25 (October 1961), 374-375.

7. Norton Stoler, Client Likability: A Variable in the Study of Psychotherapy, *Journal of Consulting Psychology* 27 (April 1963), 178.

8. Leslie D. Weatherhead, *Psychology, Religion, and Healing* (London: Hodder and Stoughton, 1952), 258.

9. Freud, *Standard Edition of the Complete Psychological Works,* 12:162-163.

10. Ibid., 12:166-167.

Chapter 9

1. Lester H. Bellwood, "Transference Phenomena in Pastoral Work" (PhD Diss., Boston University, 1962), 7.

2. James N. Kvale and Richard Dayringer, The Transference Phenomenon in the Care of the Elderly Patient, *Family Medicine* 19(2) (March-April 1987), 141-143.

3. Ronald R. Lee, *Clergy and Clients: The Practice of Pastoral Psychotherapy* (New York: Seabury, 1980), 89.

4. Edgar Draper, *Psychiatry and Pastoral Care* (Englewood Cliffs, NJ: Prentice-Hall, 1965), 79.

5. Carl R. Rogers, *Client-Centered Therapy* (Boston: Houghton Mifflin, 1951), 201.

6. Robert A. Harper, *Psychoanalysis and Psychotherapy: 36 Systems* (New York: Jason Aronson, 1974), 90-91.

7. Bellwood, "Transference Phenomena in Pastoral Work," 193-194.

8. Ibid., 7.

9. Henrich Racker, The Meanings and Uses of Countertransference, *Psychoanalytic Quarterly* 25 (July 1957), 315.

10. William U. Snyder and June B. Snyder, *The Psychotherapy Relationship* (New York: Macmillan, 1961), 342.

11. Judd Marmer, Doctor-Patient Relationship in Therapy, *American Journal of Psychoanalysis* 15(1) (1955), 8.

12. Snyder and Snyder, *The Psychotherapy Relationship,* 254-255.

Chapter 10

1. Quoted by Ross Snyder, A Ministry of Meanings and Relationship, *Pastoral Psychology* 2 (December 1960), 171.

2. Wayne E. Oates, *The Christian Pastor* (Philadelphia: Westminster, 1964), 211-212.

3. Leslie D. Weatherhead, *Psychology, Religion, and Healing* (London: Hodder and Stoughton, 1952), 339-341.

4. Carroll A. Wise, *Pastoral Counseling: Its Theory and Practice* (New York: Harper Brothers, 1951), 155.

5. Edward E. Thornton, *Theology and Pastoral Counseling* (Englewood Cliffs, NJ: Prentice-Hall, 1964), 34-35.

6. Wayne E. Oates, ed., *An Introduction to Pastoral Counseling* (Nashville: Broadman, 1959), 211.

7. Wayne E. Oates, *The Bible in Pastoral Care* (Philadelphia: Westminster, 1953), 113-114, 118-119.

8. Ibid.

9. Donald Capps, *Biblical Approaches to Pastoral Counseling* (Philadelphia: Westminster, 1981), 17-46.

10. Seward Hiltner, *Pastoral Counseling* (Nashville: Abingdon, 1949), 202.

11. William E. Hulme, *Counseling and Theology* (Philadelphia: Muhlenberg, 1956), 223-224.

Chapter 11

1. L. L. Weed, *Medical Records, Medical Education and Patient Care* (Cleveland, OH: The Press of Case Western Reserve University, 1969); A. Feinstein, The Problems of the "Problem-Oriented Medical Record," *Annals Internal Medicine* 1973, 78 (1973), 751-762.

2. R. L. Grant and B. M. Maletzki, Application of the Weed System to Psychiatric Records, *Psychiatry in Medicine* 3 (1972), 119-129; P. D. McLean and J. E. Miles, Evaluation and the Problem-Oriented Record in Psychiatry, *Archives of General Psychiatry* 31 (1974), 622-625; R. Ryback, *The Problem-Oriented Record in Psychiatry and Mental Health Care* (New York: Grune and Stratton, 1974), 4.

3. R. Ryback and J. Gardner, Problem Definition: The Problem-Oriented Record, *American Journal of Psychiatry* 130 (1973), 312-316; R. F. Buchan, The Problem-Oriented Record, *New England Journal of Medicine* 288 (1973), 1133; M. Calder, A. Landon, M. L. Miller, and S. Volkes, How We Won the Health Team's Support for P.O.M.R., *Nursing* 11(4) (April 1981), 137-142.

4. Pearl S. Berman, *Case Conceptualization and Treatment Planning* (Thousand Oaks, CA: Sage, 1997).

5. Weed, op. cit., p. 25.

6. Ibid., p. 25.

7. Grant and Maletzki, op. cit.

Chapter 12

1. Harry Stack Sullivan, *The Psychiatric Interview,* edited by Helen Swick Perry and Mary Ladd Gawel (New York: W. W. Norton, 1954), 223.

2. Ibid., 41.

3. Otto Rank, *Will Therapy and Truth and Reality,* translated by Jessie Taft (New York: Alfred A. Knopf, 1945), 178-179.

4. Quoted by Jerome D. Frank, The Dynamics of the Psychotherapeutic Relationship, *Psychiatry* 22 (February 1959), 23.

5. Ronald R. Lee, *Clergy and Clients: The Practice of Pastoral Psychotherapy* (New York: Seabury, 1980), 140.

6. Lawrence M. Brammer and Everett L. Shostrom, *Therapeutic Psychology* (Englewood Cliffs, NJ: Prentice-Hall, 1968), 204-205.

7. Irving B. Weiner, *Principles of Psychotherapy* (New York: John Wiley, 1975), 288.

8. Karl Menninger and Philip S. Holzman, *Theory of Psychoanalytic Technique,* second edition (New York: Basic Books, 1973), 178.

9. C. W. Brister, *Pastoral Care in the Church,* third edition (New York: Harper and Row, 1992), 202.

10. Charles V. Gerkin, *The Living Human Document: Re-Visioning Pastoral Counseling in a Hermeneutical Mode* (Nashville: Abingdon, 1984), 190.

PART III

1. Paul E. Johnson, *Psychology of Pastoral Care* (Nashville: Abingdon, 1953), 69-102.

Chapter 13

1. Leslie E. Moser, *Counseling: A Modern Emphasis in Religion* (Englewood Cliffs, NJ: Prentice-Hall, 1962), 229-230.

2. Sigmund Freud, *The Standard Edition of the Complete Psychological Works of Sigmund Freud,* translated and edited by James Strachey, 24 volumes (London: Hogarth, 1955-1961), 11:51.

3. Seward Hiltner, *The Counselor in Counseling* (Nashville: Abingdon, 1952), 10.

4. C. W. Brister, *Pastoral Care in the Church,* third edition (New York: Harper and Row, 1992), 171-172.

5. Donald M. Taylor, Changes in the Self Concept Without Psychotherapy, *Journal of Consulting Psychology* 19 (June 1955), 208.

6. Freud, *Standard Edition of the Complete Psychological Works,* 12:125.

7. Theodore Reik, *Listening with the Third Ear* (New York: Grove, 1948), 128.

8. Henry E. Kagan, lecture notes, postgraduate course on medicine and religion (University of Kansas, School of Medicine, 1965, mimeographed).

9. Hiltner, *The Counselor in Counseling,* 147-148.

10. Irving B. Weiner, *Principles of Psychotherapy* (New York: John Wiley, 1975), 56.

11. Valerian J. Derlega, Susan S. Hendick, Barbara A. Winstead, and John H. Berg, *Psychotherapy as a Personal Relationship* (New York: Guilford, 1991), 4.

12. Carl R. Rogers, *Client-Centered Therapy* (Boston: Houghton Mifflin, 1951), 199-200.

13. E. H. Porter, Jr., *An Introduction to Therapeutic Counseling* (New York: Houghton Mifflin, 1950), 162-163.

14. I. Haug and C. Alexander, "Dual Relationship Issues Among Clergy Therapists," in G.W. Brock, ed., *Ethics Casebook* (New York: AAMFT, 1994).

15. William U. Snyder and June B. Snyder, *The Psychotherapy Relationship* (New York: Macmillan, 1961), 225.

16. Seward Hiltner and Lowell G. Colston, *The Context of Pastoral Counseling* (Nashville: Abingdon, 1961), 38-39.

17. Karl Menninger and Philip S. Holzman, *Theory of Psychoanalytic Technique,* second edition (New York: Basic Books, 1973), 33.

18. Hiltner and Colston, *The Context of Pastoral Counseling,* 39-40.

19. Jules H. Masserman, *The Practice of Dynamic Psychiatry* (Philadelphia: W. B. Saunders, 1955), 567.

20. William R. Miller and Kathleen A. Jackson, *Practical Psychology for Pastors* (Englewood Cliffs, NJ: Prentice-Hall, 1985), 375.

Chapter 14

1. Thomas W. Klink, *Depth Perspectives in Pastoral Work* (Englewood Cliffs, NJ: Prentice-Hall, 1965), 37-38, 66.

2. Carroll A. Wise, *Pastoral Counseling: Its Theory and Practice* (New York: Harper Brothers, 1951), 63.

3. Rollo May, *The Art of Counseling,* revised edition (New York: Gardner, 1989), 120.

4. Carl R. Rogers, A Physician-Patient or Therapist-Client Relationship? in *Psychology, Psychiatry, and the Public Interest,* edited by Maurice H. Krent (Minneapolis: University of Minnesota Press, 1956), 40.

5. F. E. Fiedler, The Concept of an Ideal Therapeutic Relationship, *Journal of Consulting Psychology* 14 (August 1950), 244.

6. Edgar Draper, *Psychiatry and Pastoral Care* (Englewood Cliffs, NJ: Prentice-Hall, 1965), 61-63.

7. Paul E. Johnson, *Psychology of Pastoral Care* (Nashville: Abingdon, 1953), 34.

8. Arnold Buchheimer and Sarah Carter Balogh, *The Counseling Relationship: A Casebook* (Chicago: Science Research Associates, 1961), 9-10.

9. Heiie Faber and Ebel van der Schoot, *The Art of Pastoral Conversation* (Nashville: Abingdon, 1965), 175.

10. C. W. Brister, *Pastoral Care in the Church,* third edition (New York: Harper and Row, 1992), 73.

11. Ibid., 187.

12. Russell L. Dicks, *Pastoral Work and Personal Counseling* (New York: Macmillan, 1957), 30.

13. Wayne E. Oates, *The Christian Pastor* (Philadelphia: Westminster, 1964), 148-149.

14. Richard Dayringer, Problems in Communicating the Gospel, *Quarterly Review* 25 (April 1965), 42.

15. Charles Duell Kean, *Christian Faith and Pastoral Care* (Greenwich, CT: Seabury, 1961), 29-30.

16. Brister, *Pastoral Care in the Church,* third edition (New York: Harper, 1992), 160.

17. Wise, *Pastoral Counseling: Its Theory and Practice,* 169.

Bibliography

Allen, F. H. *Psychotherapy with Children.* New York: W. W. Norton, 1942.

American Association of Pastoral Counselors. *Handbook.* New York: American Association of Pastoral Counselors, 1972.

American Psychiatric Association. *Diagnostic and Statistical Manual of Mental Disorders,* fourth edition. Washington, DC: American Psychiatric Association, 1994.

Anderson, H. *The Family and Pastoral Care.* Philadelphia: Fortress, 1984.

Ansbacher, H. L. and Ansbacher, R. R. *The Individual Psychology of Alfred Adler.* New York: Basic Books, 1956.

Augsburger, D. *Caring Enough to Confront.* Ventura, CA: Regal, 1980.

Bardill, Donald R. *The Relational Systems Model for Family Therapy.* New York: The Haworth Press, 1997.

Barnard, E. You and Your Relationship. *Church Administration* (November 1967), 12-14.

Becker, A. H. "The Function of Relationship in Pastoral Counseling." PhD Diss., Boston University, 1958.

Bellwood, L. H. "Transference Phenomena in Pastoral Work." PhD Diss., Boston University, 1962.

Berenson, B. G. and Carkhuff, R. R. *Sources of Gain in Counseling and Psychotherapy.* New York: Holt, Rinehart and Winston, 1967.

Berman, Pearl S. *Case Conceptualization and Treatment Planning.* Thousand Oaks, CA: Sage, 1977.

Black, J. D. Common Factors of the Patient-Therapist Relationship in Diverse Psychotherapies. *Journal of Clinical Psychology* 8 (July 1952), 302-306.

Bown, O. H. "An Investigation of Therapeutic Relationships in Client-Centered Psychotherapy." PhD Diss., University of Chicago, 1954.

Brammer, L. M. and Shostrom, E. L. *Therapeutic Psychology.* Englewood Cliffs, NJ: Prentice-Hall, 1968.

Brister, C. W. *Pastoral Care in the Church.* New York: Harper and Row, 1964, revised edition, 1977; third edition, 1992.

Browning, D. S. *Atonement and Psychotherapy.* Philadelphia: Westminister, 1966.

————. *The Moral Context of Pastoral Care.* Philadelphia: Westminster, 1976.

Buber, M. *I and Thou.* Translated by Walter Kaufman and G. S. Smith. New York: Scribner's, 1970.

Buchheimer, A. and Balogh, S. C. *The Counseling Relationship: A Casebook.* Chicago: Science Research Associates, 1961.

Campbell, R. J. *Psychiatric Dictionary,* fifth edition. New York: Oxford University Press, 1981.

Capps, D. *Biblical Approaches to Pastoral Counseling.* Philadelphia: Westminster, 1981.

Carkhuff, R. R. *Helping and Human Relations: A Primer for Lay and Professional Helpers,* volume 1, *Selection and Training,* volume 2, *Practice and Research.* New York: Holt, Rinehart and Winston, 1969.

Carkhuff, R. R. and Berenson, B. G. *Beyond Counseling and Therapy.* New York: Holt, Rinehart and Winston, 1967.

Cashdan, S. *Object Relations Therapy: Using the Relationship.* New York: Norton, 1988.

Clinebell, H. *Basic Types of Pastoral Care and Counseling,* revised edition. Nashville: Abingdon Press, 1984.

Coleman, I. V. Patient-Physician Relationships in Psychotherapy. *American Journal of Psychiatry* 104 (April 1948), 638-641.

Dayringer, R. A Learning Theory Approach to Pastoral Counseling. *Pastoral Psychology* 20 (March 1969), 39-43.

————. ed. *Dealing with Depression: Five Pastoral Interventions.* Binghamton, NY: The Haworth Press, 1995.

————. ed. The Problem-Oriented Record in Pastoral Counseling. *Religion and Health* 17(1) (1978), 39-47.

————. ed. Problems in Communicating the Gospel. *Quarterly Review* 25 (April 1965), 35-45, 78.

————. ed. Relationship—The Chaplain's Basic Tool. *American Protestant Hospital Association Bulletin* 30 (January 1967), 11, 23-25.

————. ed. "A Study of the Relationship in Pastoral Counseling." ThD Diss., New Orleans Baptist Theological Seminary, 1968.

Derlega, V. J., Hendrick, S. S., Winstead, B. A., and Berg, J. H. *Psychotherapy as a Personal Relationship.* New York: Guilford, 1991.

Dicks, R. L. *Pastoral Work and Personal Counseling.* New York: Macmillan, 1957.

Dittes, J. E. Galvanic Skin Response as a Measure of Patient's Reaction to Therapist's Permissiveness. *Journal of Abnormal Psychology* 55 (November 1957), 295-303.

Doherty, W. J. *Soul Searching: Why Psychotherapy Must Promote Moral Responsibility.* New York: BasicBooks/HarperCollins, 1995.

Draper, E. *Psychiatry and Pastoral Care.* Englewood Cliffs, NJ: Prentice-Hall, 1965.

Durkin, H. M. Dr. John Levy's Relationship Therapy as Applied to a Play Group. *American Journal of Orthopsychiatry* 9 (July 1939), 583-597.

Eaton, J. W. The Client-Practitioner Relationship as a Variable in the Evaluation of Treatment Outcome. *Psychiatry* 22 (May 1959), 189-195.

Elinson, I., Padilla, E., and Perkins, M. *Public Image of Mental Health Services.* New York: Mental Health Materials Center, 1967.

Ellens, J. H. *God's Grace and Human Health.* Nashville: Abingdon, 1982.

Estadt, B. K., ed. *Pastoral Counseling.* Englewood Cliffs, NJ: Prentice-Hall, 1983.

Estes, S. G. Concerning the Therapeutic Relationship in the Dynamics of Cure. *Journal of Consulting Psychology* 12 (March 1948), 76-81.

Faber, H. and van der Schoot, E. *The Art of Pastoral Conversation.* Nashville: Abingdon, 1965.

Farson, R. E. Introjection in the Psychotherapeutic Relationship. *Journal of Consulting Pscyhology* 8 (Winter 1961), 337-343.

Feltham, Coun. ed. *Which Psychotherapy?* Thousand Oaks, CA: Sage, 1997.

Fielder, F. E. "A Comparative Investigation of Early Therapeutic Relationships." PhD Diss., University of Chicago, 1949.

————. A Comparison of Therapeutic Relationship in Psychoanalytic, Nondirective, and Adlerian Therapy. *Journal of Consulting Psychology* 14 (December 1950), 436-445.

————. The Concept of an Ideal Therapeutic Relationship. *Journal of Consulting Psychology* 14 (August 1950), 239-245.

Frank, J. D. The Demoralized Mind. *Psychology Today* 6 (April 1973), 22, 26, 28, 31, 100-101.

————. The Dynamics of the Psychotherapeutic Relationship. *Psychiatry* 22 (February 1959), 17-29.

————. *Persuasion and Healing: A Comparative Study of Psychotherapy,* revised edition. Baltimore: Johns Hopkins, 1973.

Freud, S. *The Standard Edition of the Complete Pscyhological Works of Sigmund Freud.* Translated and edited by James Strachey, 24 volumes. London: Hogarth, 1955-1961.

Fromm-Reichmann, F. *Principles of Intensive Psychotherapy.* Chicago: University of Chicago Press, 1950.

Garfield, S. L. and Bergin, A. E. eds., *Handbook of Psychotherapy and Behavior Change,* third edition. New York: Wiley, 1986.

Gelso, C. J. and Carter, J. A. The Relationship in Counseling and Psychotherapy: Components, Consequences, and Theoretical Antecedents. *The Counseling Psychologist, 13* (1985) 155-243.

Gerkin, C. V. *The Living Human Document: Re-Visioning Pastoral Counseling in a Hermeneutical Mode.* Nashville: Abingdon, 1984.

Guerney, B. G., Jr. *Relationship Enhancement.* Washington: Jossey-Bass, 1977.

Gurman, A. S. and Kniskern, D. P., eds. *Handbook of Family Therapy.* New York: Brunner/Mazel, 1991.

Harper, R. A. *Psychoanalysis and Psychotherapy: 36 Systems.* New York: Jason Aronson, 1974.

Haug, I. and Alexander, C. *Ethics Casebook.* New York: AAMFT, 1994.

Heine, R. W. "An Investigation of the Relationship Between Change and the Responsible Factors as Seen by Psychotherapists of the Psychoanalytic, Adlerian, and Non-Directive Schools." PhD Diss., University of Chicago, 1950.

Heller, K. and Goldstein, A. P. Client Dependency and Therapist Expectancy as Relationship Maintaining Variables in Psychotherapy. *Journal of Consulting Psychology* 25 (October 1961), 371-375.

Herink, R., ed. *The Psychology Handbook.* New York: New American Library, 1980.

Hiler, E. W. An Analysis of Patient-Therapist Compatability. *Journal of Consulting Psychology* 23 (October 1958), 341-346.

Hiltner, S. *The Counselor in Counseling.* Nashville: Abingdon, 1952.

————. *Pastoral Counseling.* Nashville: Abingdon, 1949.

————. *Theological Dynamics.* Nashville: Abingdon, 1972.

Hiltner, S. and Colston, L. G. *The Context of Pastoral Counseling.* Nashville: Abingdon, 1961.

Holifield, E. B. *A History of Pastoral Care in America.* Nashville: Abingdon, 1983.

Holy Bible, New Revised Standard Version. Division of Christian Education of the National Council of Churches of Christ in the U.S.A., 1989.

Hulme, W. E. *Counseling and Theology.* Philadelphia: Muhlenberg, 1956.

Hutchins, D. E. and Cole, C. G. *Helping Relationships and Strategies.* Monterey, CA: Brooks/Cole, 1986.

Ingham, H. V. and Love, L. R. *The Process of Psychotherapy.* New York: McGraw-Hill, 1954.

Jackson, E. N. *The Pastor and His People.* Manhasset, NY: Channel, 1963.

Johnson, P. E. *Person and Counselor.* Nashville: Abingdon, 1967.

————. *Psychology of Pastoral Care.* Nashville: Abingdon, 1953.

————. *Psychology of Religion.* Nashville: Abingdon, 1959.

Joint Commission of Mental Illness and Health. *Action for Mental Health.* New York: Basic, 1961.

Jongsma, A. E., Jr., Peterson, M., and McInnis, W. P. *The Child and Adolescent Psychotherapy Treatment Planner.* New York: Wiley, 1996.

Jung, C. G. *The Practice of Psychotherapy.* Edited by H. Read, M. Fordham, and G. Adler, 16 volumes. New York: Pantheon, 1953-1961.

Kagan, H. E. "Lecture notes." Postgraduate course on Medicine and Religion. University of Kansas, School of Medicine, 1965. Mimeograph.

Kahn, M. *Between Therapist and Client: The New Relationship.* New York: Freeman, 1991; revised edition, 1997.

Kean, C. D. *Christian Faith and Pastoral Care.* Greenwich, CT: Seabury, 1961.

Kelly, E. W., Jr. *Relationship-Centered Counseling.* New York: Springer, 1994.

Klink, T. W. *Depth Perspectives in Pastoral Work.* Englewood Cliffs, NJ: Prentice-Hall, 1965.

Kohut, H. *How Does Analysis Cure?* Chicago: University of Chicago, 1984.

Kottler, J. A., Sexton, T. L., and Whiston, S. C. *The Heart of Healing: Relationships in Therapy.* New York: Jossey-Bass, 1994.

Kvale, J. N. and Dayringer, R. The Transference Phenomenon in the Care of Elderly Patients. *Family Medicine* 19(2), (March-April 1987), 141-143.

Larson, R. F. The Clergyman's Role in the Therapeutic Process: Disagreement Between Clergymen and Psychiatrists. *Psychiatry* 31 (1968), 250-263.

Lee, R. R. *Clergy and Clients: The Practice of Pastoral Psychotherapy.* New York: Seabury, 1980.

Levy, J. Relationship Therapy. *American Journal of Orthopsychiatry* 8 (January 1938), 64-69.

Marmer, J. Doctor-Patient Relationship in Therapy. *American Journal of Psychoanalysis* 15(1) (1955), 7-9.

Masserman, J. H. *The Practice of Dynamic Psychaitry.* Philadelphia: W. B. Saunders, 1955.

May, R. *The Art of Counseling.* New York: Abingdon-Cokesbury, 1939; revised edition. New York: Gardner, 1989.

May, W. F. Code, Covenant, Contract, or Philanthropy. *Hastings Center Report* 5 (December 1975), 29-38.

McHolland, J. *The Future of Pastoral Counseling.* Fairfax, VA: AAPC, 1993.

McNeill, J. T. *A History of the Cure of Souls.* New York: Harper Brothers, 1951.

Menninger, K. and Holzman, P. S. *Theory of Pscyhoanalytic Technique,* second edition. New York: Basic, 1973.

Miller, W. R. and Jackson, K. A. *Practical Pscyhology for Pastors.* Englewood Cliffs, NJ: Prentice-Hall, 1985.

Minuchin, S. *Families and Family Therapy.* Cambridge: Harvard University Press, 1974.

Moser, L. E. *Counseling: A Modern Emphasis in Religion.* Englewood Cliffs, NJ: Prentice-Hall, 1962.

Moustakas, Clark. *Relationship Play Therapy.* New York: Aronson, 1997.

Moy, C. T. "Touch in the Therapeutic Relationship: An Exploratory Study with Therapists Who Touch." PhD Diss., Southern Illinois University, 1980.

Mudd, E. H. and Krich, A., eds. *Man and Wife.* New York: W. W. Norton, 1957.

Nichols, M. P. and Schwartz, R. C. *Family Therapy: Concepts and Methods.* Boston: Allyn and Bacon, 1991.

Norcross, J. C., ed. *Handbook of Eclectic Psychotherapy.* New York: Brunner/Mazel, 1986.

Norcross, J. C. and Goldfried, M. R. *Handbook of Psychotherapy Integration.* New York: Basic Books, 1992.

Noyce, G. *The Art of Pastoral Counseling.* Atlanta: John Knox, 1981.

Oates, W. E. *The Bible in Pastoral Care.* Philadelphia: Westminster, 1953.

————. *The Christian Pastor.* Philadelphia: Westminster, 1964.

————. *An Introduction to Pastoral Counseling.* Nashville: Broadman, 1959.

————. *The Presence of God in Pastoral Counseling.* Waco, TX: Word, 1986.

————. *Protestant Pastoral Counseling.* Philadelphia: Westminster, 1962.

Oates, W. E., ed. The Findings of the Commission on the Ministry. *Annals of the New York Academy of Sciences* 63 (November 1955), 415-417.

Oglesby, W. B., Jr. *Biblical Themes for Pastoral Care.* Nashville: Abingdon, 1980.

Palmer, Stephen and Varmo, Ved, eds. *The Future of Counseling and Psychotherapy.* Thousand Oaks, CA: Sage, 1997.

Parloff, M. B. "Some Factors Affecting the Quality of Therapeutic Relationships." *Journal of Abnormal and Social Psychology* (January 1956), 5-10.

Patterson, C. H. *Relationship Counseling and Psychotherapy.* New York: Harper and Row, 1974.

Patterson, C. H. and Hildare, S. C. *Successful Psychotherapy: A Caring, Loving Relationship.* Northvale, NJ: Jason Aronson, 1997.

————. *The Therapeutic Relationship: Foundations for an Eclectic Psychotherapy.* Monterey, CA: Brooks/Cole, 1986.

Patton, J. *Pastoral Counseling: A Ministry of the Church.* Nashville: Abingdon, 1983.

Perlman, H. H. *Relationship: The Heart of Helping People.* Chicago: University of Chicago Press, 1979.

Perls, F. *Gestalt Therapy Verbatim.* New York: Bantam, 1969.

Pfister, O. *Christianity and Fear.* London: Allen and Unwin, 1948.

Porter, E. H., Jr. *An Introduction to Therapeutic Counseling.* New York: Houghton Mifflin, 1950.

Pruyser, P. *The Minister as Diagnostician: Personal Problems in Pastoral Perspective.* Philadelphia: Westminster, 1976.

Quinn, R. D. "Psychotherapists' Expression as an Index to the Quality of Early Therapeutic Relationships Established by Representatives of the Nondirective, Adlerian and Psychoanalystic Schools." PhD Diss., University of Chicago.

Racker, H. The Meanings and Uses of Countertransference. *Psychoanalytic Quarterly* 25 (July 1957), 302-357.

————. *Transference and Countertransference.* New York: International Universities Press, 1968.

Ramsey, G. V. The Initial Counseling Interview. *Pastoral Psychology* 17 (November 1966), 27-34.

Rank, O. *Will Therapy and Truth and Reality.* Translated by Jessie Taft. New York: Knopf, 1945.

Reik, T. *Listening With the Third Ear.* New York: Grove, 1948.

Rogers, C. R. "A Physician-Patient or Therapist-Client Relationship?" In *Psychology, Psychiatry, and the Public Interest,* edited by Maurice H. Krent. Minneapolis: University of Minnesota Press, 1956.

————. *Client-Centered Therapy.* Boston: Houghton Mifflin, 1951.

————. *The Clinical Treatment of the Problem Child.* Boston: Houghton Mifflin, 1939.

————. *Counseling and Psychotherapy.* Boston: Houghton Mifflin, 1942.

————. *On Becoming a Person.* Boston: Houghton Mifflin, 1961.

Rogers, C. R., ed. *The Therapeutic Relationship and Its Impact.* Westport, CT: Greenwood, 1967.

Rubenstein, E. A. and Parloff, M. B., eds. *Research in Psychotherapy.* Washington: American Psychological Association, 1959.

Schofield, W. *Psychotherapy: The Purchase of Friendship.* Englewood Cliffs, NJ: Prentice-Hall, 1964.

Smith, D. Trends in Counseling and Psychotherapy. *American Psychologist* 37 (1982), 802-809.

Snyder, R. A. Ministry of Meanings and Relationships. *Pastoral Psychology* (December 1960), 18-24.

Snyder, W. U. and Snyder, J. B. *The Psychotherapy Relationship.* New York: Macmillan, 1961.

Standal, S. W. and Corsini, R. J., eds. *Critical Incidents in Psychotherapy.* Englewood Cliffs, NJ: Prentice-Hall, 1959.

Steinzor, B. *The Healing Partnership.* New York: Harper and Row, 1967.

Stewart, C. Relationship Counseling. *Journal of Pastoral Care* 13 (Winter 1959), 209-220.

Stewart, C. W. *The Minister as Marriage Counselor,* revised edition. New York: Abingdon, 1970.

Stoler, N. Client Likability: A Variable in the Study of Psychotherapy. *Journal of Consulting Psychology* 27 (April 1963), 175-178.

Stone, H. W. *Using Behavioral Methods in Pastoral Counseling.* Philadelphia: Fortress, 1980.

Sullivan, H. S. *The Psychiatric Interview.* Edited by Helen Swick Perry and Mary Ladd Gawel. New York: W. W. Norton, 1954.

————. *The Interpersonal Theory of Psychiatry.* New York: W. W. Norton, 1953.

Sundland, D. M. and Barker, E. N. The Orientations of Psychotherapists. *Journal of Consulting Psychology* 4 (April 1962), 201-212.

Taft, J. *The Dynamics of Therapy in a Controlled Relationship.* New York: Macmillan, 1933.

Taylor, D. M. Changes in the Self Concept Without Psychotherapy. *Journal of Consulting Psychology* 19 (June 1955), 205-209.

Thomas, Zachary. *Healing Touch: The Church's Forgotten Language.* Louisville: Westminster/John Knox, 1994.

Thorne, F. C. *Principles of Personality Counseling.* Brandon, VT: Journal of Clinical Psychology, 1950.

Thornton, E. E. *Theology and Pastoral Counseling.* Englewood Cliffs, NJ: Prentice-Hall, 1964.

Truax, C. B. and Carkhuff, R. R. *Toward Effective Counseling and Psychotherapy: Training and Practice.* Chicago: Adeline, 1967.

Tyler, L. E. *The Work of the Counselor.* New York: Appleton-Century-Crofts, 1953.

Valerian, J. D., Hendrick, S. S., Winstead, B. A., and Berg, J. H. *Psychotherapy as a Personal Relationship.* New York: Guilford, 1991.

Van Deusen, D. G. *Redemptive Counseling.* Richmond, VA: John Knox, 1960.

Veroff, J., Kulka, R. S., and Douvan, E. *Mental Health in America: Patterns of Seeking Help From 1957 to 1976.* New York: Basic, 1981.

Vorhaus, M. G. *The Changing Patient-Doctor Relationship.* New York: Horizon, 1957.

Wallis, J. H. *Personal Counselling: An Introduction to Relationship Therapy.* London: Allen and Unwin, 1973.

Waskow, I. E. Counselor Attitudes and Client Behavior. *Journal of Consulting Psychology* 27 (October 1963), 405-412.

Weatherhead, L. D. *Psychology, Religion, and Healing.* London: Hodder and Stoughton, 1952.

Weiner, I. B. *Principles of Psychotherapy.* New York: John Wiley, 1975.

Whitehorn, J. C. and Betz, B. J. A Comparison of Psychotherapeutic Relationships Between Physicians and Schizophrenic Patients When Insulin Is Combined With Psychotherapy and When Psychotherapy Is Used Alone. *American Journal of Psychiatry* 113 (April 1957), 901-910.

Wicks, R. J., Parsons, R. D., and Capps, D., eds. *Clinical Handbook of Pastoral Counseling,* volume 1, expanded edition. New York: Paulist, 1985.

Wicks, R. J. and Parsons, R. D., eds. *Clinical Handbook of Pastoral Counseling,* volume 2. Mahwah, NJ: Paulist, 1993.

Wilson, J. M. The Value of Touch in Psychotherapy. *American Journal of Orthopsychiatry* 52(1) (1982), 65-72.

Wise, C. A. *Pastoral Counseling: Its Theory and Practice.* New York: Harper Brothers, 1951.

———. *Pastoral Psychotherapy.* New York: Jason Aronson, 1983.

Wolberg, L. R. *The Technique of Psychotherapy.* New York: Grune and Stratton, 1954.

Wolstein, B. *Transference.* New York: Grune and Stratton, 1964.

Wynn, J. C. *Family Therapy in Pastoral Ministry.* New York: Harper and Row, 1982.

Yalom, I. D. *Existential Psychothrapy.* New York: Basic Books, 1980.

Yoder, W. H. The Place of Relationship in Learning How to Pray. *Pastoral Psychology* 12 (April 1961), 39-42.

Index

Page numbers followed by the letter "f" indicate figures.

Order Your Own Copy of
This Important Book for Your Personal Library!

THE HEART OF PASTORAL COUNSELING
Healing Through Relationship, Revised Edition

_____ in hardbound at $39.95 (ISBN: 0-7890-0172-1)

_____ in softbound at $19.95 (ISBN: 0-7890-0421-6)

COST OF BOOKS_____

OUTSIDE USA/CANADA/
MEXICO: ADD 20%_____

POSTAGE & HANDLING_____
*(US: $3.00 for first book & $1.25
for each additional book)
Outside US: $4.75 for first book
& $1.75 for each additional book)*

SUBTOTAL_____

IN CANADA: ADD 7% GST_____

STATE TAX_____
*(NY, OH & MN residents, please
add appropriate local sales tax)*

FINAL TOTAL_____
*(If paying in Canadian funds,
convert using the current
exchange rate. UNESCO
coupons welcome.)*

☐ **BILL ME LATER:** ($5 service charge will be added)
(Bill-me option is good on US/Canada/Mexico orders only;
not good to jobbers, wholesalers, or subscription agencies.)

☐ Check here if billing address is different from
shipping address and attach purchase order and
billing address information.

Signature_____

☐ **PAYMENT ENCLOSED: $**_____

☐ **PLEASE CHARGE TO MY CREDIT CARD.**

☐ Visa   ☐ MasterCard   ☐ AmEx   ☐ Discover
☐ Diners Club
Account # _____

Exp. Date _____

Signature _____

Prices in US dollars and subject to change without notice.

NAME _____

INSTITUTION _____

ADDRESS _____

CITY _____

STATE/ZIP _____

COUNTRY _____ COUNTY (NY residents only) _____

TEL _____ FAX _____

E-MAIL_____

May we use your e-mail address for confirmations and other types of information? ☐ Yes   ☐ No

Order From Your Local Bookstore or Directly From
The Haworth Press, Inc.
10 Alice Street, Binghamton, New York 13904-1580 • USA
TELEPHONE: 1-800-HAWORTH (1-800-429-6784) / Outside US/Canada: (607) 722-5857
FAX: 1-800-895-0582 / Outside US/Canada: (607) 772-6362
E-mail: getinfo@haworth.com
PLEASE PHOTOCOPY THIS FORM FOR YOUR PERSONAL USE.

BOF96